Meani... W9-CAG-578

Meaning

A SLIM GUIDE TO SEMANTICS

Paul Elbourne

OXFORD

UNIVERSITY PRESS

OXFORD

UNIVERSITY PRESS

Great Clarendon Street, Oxford OX2 6DP
United Kingdom

Oxford University Press is a department of the University of Oxford.
It furthers the University's objective of excellence in research, scholarship,
and education by publishing worldwide. Oxford is a registered trade mark of
Oxford University Press in the UK and in certain other countries

First published 2011
Reprinted 2013

British Library Cataloguing in Publication Data
Data available

Library of Congress Cataloging in Publication Data
Data available

ISBN 978-0-19-969662-8

To Síofra

Contents

Preface

The ability to communicate linguistically with each other in the extraordinarily rich way that we do is a distinguishing feature of the human species. To communicate linguistically is to convey meaning. This book offers an introduction to semantics, the discipline that analyses meaning. Semantics asks questions like

'What is meaning?',

'How do meanings of words combine with each other to give us meanings of sentences?',

and

'Do the meanings of the words in our languages influence what thoughts we can think?' All of these questions will be addressed in this book.

To be precise, this book is about natural language semantics, which is the analysis of the meanings of words and sentences in natural languages like English and Japanese. It will have nothing to say about the semantics of computer programming languages and other artificial languages, important though that topic is. And it will regrettably have nothing to say about the meaning of life, important though that topic arguably is too. Natural language semantics is a peculiar discipline in that it is carried out under the collective aegis of three larger subjects: linguistics, psychology, and philosophy. This book looks at theories from all three. Semantics is also notable for the amount of controversy involved, on everything from small details to the most basic foundations of the field. Unlike some other introductory texts, this book will not shy away from exploring disagreements and difficulties.

I am very grateful to John Davey, of OUP, for his encouragement and for all kinds of advice; to Lera Boroditsky for confirming some details of her experiments; and to Joanne Dixon, Lee Jackson, and Síofra Pierse for reading various drafts of the manuscript and telling me what was incomprehensible and what was not.

1

Definitions

Words are traditionally supposed to have meanings. Indeed it is widely supposed to be possible to *define* words' meanings. Whole books, called dictionaries, are devoted to listing the definitions of words; and philosophers from Socrates (469–399 BC) and Plato (429–347 BC) onwards have devoted obsessive attention to pinning down the meaning of philosophically interesting words like *knowledge, truth, justice,* and, indeed, *meaning*. It is important for anyone embarking upon the study of semantics to realize, however, that defining the meaning of a word is an enterprise of almost inconceivable complexity. Despite 2,400 years or so of trying, it is unclear that anyone has ever come up with an adequate definition of any word whatsoever, even the simplest. Certainly the definitions in dictionaries are the merest hints, and are sometimes flat out wrong.

Before we look at some examples of attempted definitions, it will be useful to formulate a standard by which we might appropriately judge them. Suppose I define *chair* as 'item of furniture'. It is clear, I think, that my definition is faulty. Why? Because there are plenty of things that are items of furniture that are not chairs—tables, desks, footstools, and so on. My definition is too lax, in the sense that it includes too many things. Suppose, on the other hand, that I define *chair* as 'throne'. My definition is once again flawed. All thrones are plausibly chairs, but there are lots of chairs that are not thrones. My definition is now too strict, in the sense that it excludes too many things. A good definition of the word *chair*, it seems, must be neither too strict nor too lax; in other words, it must pick out all and only the things that are chairs. And similarly for definitions of other words.

How well do dictionary definitions of *chair* measure up on this score? Let us look at a few and find out. The *Collins Pocket English Dictionary*, one of the more respected and well known smaller dictionaries of English, in its 2008 edition, defines *chair* as 'a seat with a back and four legs, for one person to sit on'. Does this pick out all and only the things that are chairs? Why, no, it does not. If that is not immediately obvious to you, think about the chairs in which the office workers of today can be found sitting at their desks. Some people do of course use a seat with a back and four legs for this purpose. But many are to be found swivelling around in a seat that rests on one central column that splays out near ground level into five or six separate castor-bearing feet. However you do the count, you cannot plausibly impute four legs to these devices; and yet they are indubitably chairs. So this definition is too strict, in the sense that it unjustly denies chairhood to many things that merit it.

Interestingly, the definition also seems to be too lax. Think back to the Diogenes Club of the Sherlock Holmes stories, a club in which no member is allowed to take the slightest bit of notice of any other member. Imagine that it has a garden adorned with ordinary garden benches. Two or three people could easily fit on each bench. But the club rules, we can well imagine, forbid any person to sit on a bench that is already occupied by another person. These garden benches, then, are seats with a back and four legs, for one person to sit on. But they are surely not chairs. (If it is relevant, we can imagine that the designers and manufacturers of the benches knew the use to which they would be put, so that no-one ever intended that these benches would be occupied by more than one person at any time.) So the definition of *chair* in the *Collins Pocket English Dictionary* is simultaneously too strict and too lax.

Perhaps you are thinking that it is unfair to pick on a 'pocket dictionary'. Such dictionaries, if they are to have any chance of actually fitting into people's pockets, will not have the space to include all the details about leg-count and occupancy that a larger dictionary might. So let us go to the opposite extreme. The *Oxford English Dictionary*, in its second edition of 1989, comprises twenty volumes and

21,728 pages, and takes up several feet of shelf-space. Let us see what it has to say on the subject of chairs:

A seat for one person (always implying more or less of comfort and ease); now the common name for the movable four-legged seat with a rest for the back, which constitutes, in many forms of rudeness or elegance, an ordinary article of household furniture, and is also used in gardens or wherever it is usual to sit.

The format of this entry is slightly complex, in that it seems to offer two alternative definitions: the phrases that come respectively before and after the semi-colon. The 'now' is perhaps to be taken as implying some historical development of the meaning of the word. So let us concentrate on the second, more up-to-date, definition, 'the movable four-legged seat with a rest for the back, which constitutes, in many forms of rudeness or elegance, an ordinary article of household furniture, and is also used in gardens or wherever it is usual to sit'. Does this succeed in picking out all and only the chairs? No. For all its elegance of phrasing and luxuriance of detail, it makes the same mistake about four-leggedness that the *Collins Pocket English Dictionary* made.

What if we emended these definitions to allow for different numbers of legs? It is not immediately clear how we should do so. When you think about it, it becomes obvious that chairs could come with all kinds of different numbers of legs. An avant-garde designer could easily promote a three-legged chair, a five-legged chair or a 100-legged chair. (For the latter case, imagine very thin legs, perhaps arranged in a ten-by-ten grid.) And think back to the swivelling office chair that I just described. Is it accurate to describe this kind of chair as having legs at all? Not for my money. And if you need any further convincing, imagine a solid cube of wood that reaches the customary height of a chair seat when placed on the ground, and imagine that it has a back like a chair. Such an object could, in fact, be a chair; but it would definitely not have legs.

So maybe we should charitably pass over the claims about legs. What about the other components of the *OED* definition? To start at the start, we have already seen difficulties with the claim that a chair

3

is a seat for one person: it introduces an inappropriate degree of laxity into the definition since it allows the garden benches at the Diogenes Club to be chairs. We have not yet observed that this condition is also too strict. I am sure that you have in fact seen perfectly ordinary chairs with two people on them, one person sitting on the lap of the other. Does this not raise a difficulty for the idea that chairs are seats for one person? Well, we could perhaps defend the dictionary definitions on this point by offering some kind of explication of the word *for*. Perhaps *for* here means something like 'designed for'. In other words, we could claim that, even if some people do utilize chairs in the peculiarly unnecessary manner just described, what the dictionary authors are driving at here is something like the intent of the designer of the chairs: chairs would be designed for one person, even if some irresponsible types do not respect this. But imagine a society in which, whether due to decadence or thrift, all chairs are designed to support two people (perhaps they are slightly reinforced) and are in fact generally used like this. Would these items of furniture still be chairs? Of course. The very fact that I can write without contradiction about chairs that are designed to support two people shows this. There is no internal contradiction in the idea of a chair that is designed to support two people. Compare the idea of a unicycle with two wheels, which does seem genuinely self-contradictory. This is evidence that the idea of being associated with *one* of something or other does form part of the meaning of the word *unicycle*, whereas it does not form part of the meaning of the word *chair*.

The technique that I just used to argue against chairs being seats for one, frivolous though it may seem, actually bears closer examination, for there is a moral hidden here. We must not confuse the meaning of a word with details about how the things that that word designates are in fact produced or used. We can tell this because we can use our common, everyday words to describe components of the most outlandish counterfactual situations. Semanticists distinguish between the *extension* and the *intension* of a term like *chair*: roughly speaking, the extension of *chair* is the set of all actual chairs, while the intension is the set of possible chairs, allowing for all the possibilities of bizarre science-fiction scenarios. The meaning of *chair*, whatever

4

it is, allows us to talk not only about actual chairs, but also about merely possible chairs.

The *OED* definition says that chairs are movable, which strikes me as a good generalization, but certainly not exceptionless, and almost certainly not part of the meaning of the word *chair*. Think of a daring architect who proposes a kitchen or a dining room in which the chairs are sculpted from the stone that forms the floor. There is nothing self-contradictory about the notion. If we abstract away from the *OED*'s talk of comfort, ease, rudeness, elegance and gardens, which forms part of the baroque splendour of the entry but does not increase our understanding of chairs, there are two ideas remaining: that of a seat, and that of a rest for the back. What do the *OED* authors mean by *seat*? Fortunately, we can look up the word in the *OED* and see. The most relevant sense in the article on *seat* seems to be 'Something adapted or used for sitting upon'. Now it might seem uncontroversial that chairs are things adapted or used for sitting upon. But even this is dubious, at least if the definition is taken to claim that all chairs have this property. Imagine a grand stately home open to the public. Much of the original furniture is still there, but a few chairs are missing. The owners decide to commission the construction of some chairs, replicas of the old ones, to fill in a couple of gaps around a great dining table. They do not intend that people should sit on them, however; in fact the whole ensemble is to be shut off behind a velvet rope and no-one is to be allowed to touch the chairs in question. In case it matters, we can further suppose that the designers and manufacturers know this. These chairs, then, are not adapted or used for sitting upon. And yet they are indubitably chairs.

This leaves the idea of a 'rest for the back'. If this is taken to imply that actual human backs have to touch chairs, it seems to be falsified by the scenario about the replica chairs in the manor house; and similarly if it is understood in a slightly weaker form, so as to imply only that the manufacturers or designers must intend this. It is not obvious that this phrase can be taken in any other way.

Overall, we have found that chairs do not have to have any of the properties ascribed to them by the definition of *chair* in the *Oxford*

English Dictionary. If we judge the definition as an attempt to pick out all and only the possible chairs, it fails. Other dictionaries perform no better.

Perhaps even the *OED* does not have enough space to go into all the necessary details that a good definition would require. Or perhaps its editors have not had enough time to find out what *chair* means: work on the dictionary only began in 1879, after all, which is quite recent in terms of the history of scholarship. What about philosophy? Philosophers, as I mentioned earlier, have devoted about 2,400 years to formulating the definitions of philosophically interesting words, and they can, and frequently do, devote whole books to just one such word. Have philosophers succeeded in defining a word after all this time? Not obviously. There may possibly be an accurate definition of a word lurking in some philosophical manuscript somewhere, but it is difficult to know what it might be, because there is no consensus among philosophers on any such case. On all the examples I mentioned earlier (*knowledge, truth, justice, meaning*), and many more, there is still controversy.

To get the flavour of the enterprise, let us consider the definition of *knowledge*. (Unfortunately, the word *chair* has come in for only limited philosophical analysis.) And to avoid getting tangled up in ambiguity (of which more later), let us concentrate on what is called *propositional knowledge*: knowledge that something is the case (for example, that snow is white), as opposed to knowing (or being acquainted with) a place or a person. For quite some time, it was thought that *knowledge* could be defined as 'justified true belief'. The first analysis of this kind, in fact, goes back to Plato's *Meno* (fourth century BC). Why should one think this? Well, it seems intuitively plausible that for you to know that snow is white you must at least believe it. Knowing is a kind of believing, perhaps with other conditions thrown in. Furthermore, if you know some proposition then that proposition has to be true. You cannot know that trepanning cures people of demonic possession, because it is not true that trepanning cures people of demonic possession. (Those in thrall to the intellectual charlatanry known as 'postmodernism' might seek to convince you that nothing is true. In most cases, however, the question 'So is it *true* that nothing is true?' is enough to discombobulate them.) Why not stop here and say that knowledge is true belief? The reason is that it is possible to acquire true beliefs by accident, as it were, but we feel queasy about designating such beliefs as knowledge: a madman amidst his ravings might sincerely shout out some substantive and interesting true propositions that would be no better grounded than his belief that he is Napoleon. The requirement that the belief in question be justified somehow is meant to rule out this kind of thing from qualifying as knowledge.

So matters might have rested (I am simplifying the history somewhat) had it not been for the sublimely concise Edmund Gettier. Gettier is one of the most eminent living philosophers; but, rather splendidly, his entire published *oeuvre* consists of one three-page paper, an article from 1963 called 'Is justified true belief knowledge?' The answer to the question is no. Suppose, says Gettier, that Smith and Jones have applied for the same job. Before the result of their applications is announced, two things happen: Smith counts the coins in Jones's pocket and finds that they number ten; and the president of the company assures Smith that Jones will get the job. (We are not supposed to wonder why these things happen. This is a philosophical example, not a psychological novel.) Smith thus justifiably believes that Jones is the man who will get the job and that Jones has ten coins in his pocket. Being an impeccable logician he deduces that the man who will get the job has ten coins in his pocket. Now he is surely justified in believing this latter proposition: it is a watertight deduction from two things that he is already fully justified in believing. As it happens, however, Smith, not Jones, gets the job. And unbeknownst to himself, Smith too had ten coins in his pocket at the time that he counted Jones's coins and formed his beliefs. So it turns out that his belief that the man who would get the job had ten coins in his pocket was true. And it was also justified. But it is discomfiting in the extreme to say that Smith knew that the man who would get the job had ten coins in his pocket. So not all justified true belief is knowledge. A large part of the history of epistemology since 1963 has consisted of efforts to solve the 'Gettier problem', sometimes involving attempts to add some elusive fourth

7

property to the 'justified true belief' definition of *knowledge* and sometimes veering off in other directions; but there is no consensus in the field.

Perhaps you are now expecting me to come up with dazzling definitions of *chair* and *knowledge* that remedy the above deficiencies. I am afraid I must disappoint. The aim of this exercise has been to impress upon you the extraordinary difficulty of giving adequate definitions of words, even apparently humble ones. To give you a further taste of the difficulties that arise in this kind of exercise, let us examine some surprising facts about word meaning that have been pointed out by Noam Chomsky, the founder of generative linguistics and one of the leading figures in the 'cognitive revolution' of the 1950s and 1960s, which saw the foundation of modern cognitive psychology and artificial intelligence. In the discussion of *chair*, you may have remarked upon the important role that human intentions play in defining what seems at first to be a word for a straightforward physical object. Chomsky's observation is that this phenomenon is much more widespread than you might have thought, even in the case of words that do not denote human artefacts. If tea leaves have been deposited in your local reservoir by the proper authorities as a new kind of water purifier, what comes out of your tap will still be called *water*, even if (on one way of looking at it) it is an extremely mild tea; but if someone likes their tea very mild and dips a tea bag for just a split second into a cup of pure H_2O, the resulting liquid is tea and not water, even if it is chemically identical to the stuff that comes out of the tap. And take the word *thing*, which expresses what seems in a way to be the most basic concept we have. Chomsky points out that some sticks lying on the ground constitute a thing if left there by a human being as a signal; but they are not a thing if left there randomly by a forest fire. Such subtleties abound.

Are any words immune from the kind of complications we have seen? It is sometimes thought that we might be able to give precise definitions for words from technical domains like science or mathematics. But even here things are more complicated than we might like. Take the word *metal*, for example. The following is an excerpt from a lecture on metals by the distinguished metallurgist Robert

Pond. He begins by asking the audience to come up with a definition of *metal*. Their efforts are not successful.

Well, I'll tell you something. You really don't know what a metal is. And there's a big group of people that don't know what a metal is. Do you know what we call them? Metallurgists!... Here's why metallurgists don't know what metal is. We know that a metal is an element that has metallic properties. So we start to enumerate all these properties: electrical conductivity, thermal conductivity, ductility, malleability, strength, high density. Then you say, how many of these properties does an element have to have to classify as a metal? And do you know what? We can't get metallurgists to agree. Some say three properties; some say five properties, six properties. We really don't know. So we just proceed along presuming that we are all talking about the same thing.

Even metallurgists, then, cannot agree on a definition of the word *metal*.

Perhaps *metal* is somehow too broad a term. How about *gold*? Gold is an element of the periodic table and can be pinned down, as it were, with some exactness: it is the element with atomic number 79. What if we define *gold* as 'the element with atomic number 79'? Well, one problem with that suggestion is that most people who know the word *gold* do not know that gold's atomic number is 79. The current suggestion would imply that most competent English speakers do not know the meaning of the word *gold*, which would be a rather paradoxical state of affairs. What is it, we might ask, that allows such people to use the word appropriately? If they do not know its meaning, how is it that they use it quite successfully to talk about gold? A further problem with this suggestion can be brought out with another fantastical scenario. Imagine that an evil demon has been systematically deceiving all the scientists who have ever studied gold. The demon has been making them think that gold's atomic number is 79, but actually it is something else entirely. In fact it turns out, in this scenario, that there is no element with atomic number 79. Now suppose that this remarkable state of affairs is discovered. If the word *gold* just meant nothing other than 'the element with atomic number 79', and if there were no element with atomic number 79, it would seem that scientists would be quite justified in announcing, 'There is no such thing as gold.' (Compare 'There is no such thing as the element with atomic number 79', which would be quite true under the circumstances.) But in fact, of course, they would not be justified in announcing that. What they would actually say in such a scenario would be something like 'Gold does not have atomic number 79 (but it does exist).'

We could abandon the attempt to define *gold* by means of atomic numbers and concentrate instead on visible characteristics of gold that lay people can appreciate, such as its glittery yellow colour, its ductility, and so on. But this now looks horribly similar to lexicographical attempts to define *chair* by means of number of legs, use for sitting, and so on; and we would not be surprised to find similar difficulties arising. In this case, the existence of fool's gold (iron pyrites) would make it particularly tricky to come up with a definition of this kind that would not include too much. What we would need, of course, would be some means of telling apart gold and fool's gold. How do we do that? Why, we appeal to facts about their chemical make-up such as atomic numbers. But then we are back where we started.

One could object that *metal* and *gold* are words of ordinary language that have been co-opted by science, and that the trouble we have defining them reflects this peculiar status. What about terms that were coined in the course of explicitly theoretical speculation? I am afraid that the prospects of successfully defining words like this are not much better than the prospects of defining *gold*, and for very similar reasons. Take *atom*, for example. Suppose we attempt to give some definition that sums up current thinking about atoms, such as 'unit of matter that consists of a nucleus containing one or more protons (and optionally one or more neutrons) surrounded by a cloud of electrons'. Suppose further that we can dismiss worries about people being competent to use the word but not knowing these details; the word *atom* is sufficiently recondite, we can assume, that anyone who is competent to use it knows at least this much about atoms. It is still possible that some scientific discovery should radically change our conception of atoms, meaning that this definition no longer reflected the best current understanding of them; and yet we would still almost certainly keep the word and say things like 'Atoms are not units of matter that consist of a nucleus containing one or more protons (and optionally one or more neutrons) surrounded by a cloud of electrons after all.' This is evidence that the meaning of the word *atom* is not the definition just given, or anything along similar lines; for, if it were, it would make more sense to say, 'Since atoms, by definition, are just supposed to be units of matter of the kind we have described, and since we have just discovered that there are no such units of matter, we can deduce that atoms do not exist.'

In the case of the word *atom*, this kind of wholescale revision is not just a hypothetical scenario. The English word derives from the Ancient Greek word *atomos*, which meant 'uncuttable' or 'indivisible'. Atomists, from Leucippus and Democritus in the fifth century BC down to many scientists in the nineteenth century AD, believed that there were ultimate, indivisible units of matter out of which everything else was composed. By the latter half of the nineteenth century, some particular units of matter, called *atoms*, were tentatively identified as being these ultimate, indivisible units of matter. Then came the demonstration in 1897, by the English physicist J.J. Thomson (1856–1940), that these things in fact contained smaller particles, called electrons. What happened? Scientists did not in general conclude, 'These things are not atoms after all, since they are not indivisible.' They said, in effect, 'Atoms are not indivisible after all.' So the word *atom* did not mean 'ultimate, indivisible unit of matter'.

I know of only one area where it seems likely that we have good definitions of words: mathematics. I can see nothing wrong, for example, with the statement that *prime* means 'integer greater than one that has no factors other than itself and one'. It is a matter of some intellectual interest why mathematical terms should be immune from the general chaos that surrounds definitions; but I will not attempt to address this question here.

It is appropriate, at this point, to step back and reflect on what these examples show us. All I have been trying to demonstrate is that giving definitions of words is a task of mind-boggling complexity; by reporting on the state of the art in fields such as epistemology and metallurgy, I have been trying to suggest, but not to demonstrate conclusively, that no-one has ever given an adequate definition of a word, as far as we know, with the possible exception of mathematical terms; and by discussing a couple of dictionary entries, I hope to have convinced you that dictionary entries do not generally give the meanings of words. Some of these conclusions may be surprising, if you have never studied semantics before. But it is important to realize that they are also rather limited.

To start with, the fact that it is astonishingly difficult to give definitions of words does not show that it is impossible. Even the conclusion, if I could establish it, that no-one has ever given an adequate definition of a word would not show that. Perhaps we just have to try harder and eventually we will hit on some good definitions. Or perhaps definitions of words could in principle be given—perhaps a hyper-intelligent alien race could give some, for example—but human beings are just not smart enough to do this. This last possibility, although it might, once more, strike some readers as surprising, is really not very radical. Imagine trying to explain the atomism of Democritus, or the cathode ray experiments of J.J. Thomson, to a cow. However much you explain atomism, the cow is just not going to get it. Various thinkers have pointed out that some topics could stand in the relation to us that atomism and cathode ray experiments stand in to the cow: we are just too deeply stupid to grasp them. Maybe accurate definitions of words constitute one such topic.

So much for the question of whether we can give definitions of words. But we should also address the question of what definitions of words actually are (or would be, if we could give any). In particular, if we had a completely successful definition of a word, would it be the meaning of that word? Not in a sense that would ultimately satisfy us. The problem is that when we give a scientific or philosophical account of something, we ideally want to explain the thing in question in terms of other kinds of things, things that we take to be somehow more basic. A chemist explains water as a compound of hydrogen and oxygen; a physicist explains atoms as structures involving protons, neutrons, and electrons; a philosopher explains knowledge as true, justified belief of a certain kind. (We wave our hands a little during the last few words of that sentence.) But a definition is just a string of words. It is unsatisfying, therefore, to say that the meaning of a word is a definition, because that would be to say that the meaning of a word is just more words. It would appear that we were not progressing to any explanatorily deeper level. This is not to say, however, that effort put into constructing definitions is just wasted. As we have seen, efforts of this kind can turn up intricate and sometimes surprising facts about meaning; and any theory of meaning that purported to tell us what meanings were would also ultimately have to account for these facts.

So what things could the meanings of words be? I turn to this topic in the next chapter.

2

What are word meanings?

What things could the meanings of words be? This is no place for a history of the topic. So I will concentrate for the purposes of this chapter on two ideas that have been prominent in the specialist literature for the last few decades: the referential theory of meaning and the internalist theory of meaning.

These theories make use of some occasionally unintuitive concepts from contemporary philosophy, linguistics, and psychology. Among other things, we will read in this chapter that some linguists think that languages like English and Spanish do not exist; and that some philosophers think that Santa Claus does exist. So here, to start with, is a brief overview to establish the lie of the land.

One of the main facts about language that theorists have to account for is that people are able to use it to talk about the world. Even though we can do other things with language, like write nonsense verse, a lot of what we do with it, and lot of its utility, consists in this apparent connection with the things around us. We can describe the world, ask what it is like, and even order parts of it (sentient parts, preferably) to abide by our will. The debate in this chapter focuses on the nature of this word–world relationship.

Both sides of the debate take for granted that the meanings of words are what enable them to hook up with the world. (It is not the pronunciation, for example, that is responsible.) The *referential theory of meaning* proposes the most direct mechanism: meanings of words simply are things in the world. So the word *Iceland*, for example, has as its meaning that very island, a huge chunk of rock and ice in the northern Atlantic Ocean. So once you have grasped the meaning of the word *Iceland*, you automatically know what that word picks out in the world; for the meaning of the word just is what it picks out in the world. Now this may be all well and good with a proper name, like *Iceland*. But what of other types of words? What does the word *icy* pick out, for example? Or the word *the*? The chief problem faced by the referential theory, as we will see shortly, is that in order to provide things for all these words to pick out, theorists have to posit the existence of increasingly bizarre entities in the world, including, as I said, Santa Claus and a slew of other personages whom sober reflection had previously consigned to the status of myth.

On the other side of the floor, we have the advocates of the *internalist theory of meaning*. They suggest that word meanings are most fruitfully thought of as ideas or concepts in our heads. Take a concept, such as the concept I have of Iceland. It is some psychological entity. Ultimately, if we are correct to suppose that we do our thinking with our brains, this concept of mine is presumably a structure composed out of cells inside my head. (How all this works in detail, of course, is the profoundest of mysteries.) Since the island of Iceland resembles or *falls under* this concept of mine, I use this concept to think about Iceland. And since the concept also forms part of a word (i.e. since it is the meaning of a word), I use that word, *Iceland*, to talk about Iceland. Inside your head, you presumably have a very similar concept that forms part of a very similar word, so that when you hear me say 'Iceland' your concept of Iceland is activated. As you may have noticed, this internalist way of looking at things implies that we each have our own word *Iceland*, and cannot rule out the possibility that the associated concepts are significantly different. Not everyone is happy with this, since it seems to allow drastic failures of communication.

That is the debate in a nutshell. The details that follow can appropriately be thought of as fleshing out this summary.

Let us return to the referential theory of meaning. It says that the meanings of words are things in the world, most of which are not in our heads. Meanings, according to this view, are *referents*, or things that are picked out or referred to. It is perhaps easiest to illustrate the idea with proper names. Consider a proper name such as *Elizabeth II*.

The referential theory of meaning says that the meaning of the proper name *Elizabeth II* is Elizabeth II, Defender of the Faith and Queen of Great Britain, Northern Ireland, and the British Dominions beyond the Seas. The idea is that when you say something like *Elizabeth II is wise*, the name *Elizabeth II* contributes that very woman to what you are saying; and then you say of her that she is wise. But what about the phrase *is wise* and other predicates (like *icy*)? Is there any way to find referents for them? Why, yes. The idea here is that the word *wise* refers to the *property* of being wise.

At one level, the notion of a property is familiar and homely enough. A property is an aspect or characteristic of something. This apple has the property of being red; that one has the property of being green; both have the property of being an apple. But already, in saying this much, we are entering upon controversial philosophical ground. Some philosophers have claimed that, if my red apple and my green apple both have the property of being an apple, then this implies that there is a separate thing, the property of being an apple, which both of my apples have. A property of the philosophical kind would be rather similar to a property of the commercial kind, in that both kinds of thing can be jointly possessed. Many philosophers have thought this, beginning with Plato, whose *Forms* are often taken to be forerunners of properties in this sense. Plato would have said that my red apple and my green apple separately instantiate the Form of the Apple, which is an eternal, unchanging, non-physical entity that is something like a blueprint for all earthly apples; only by instantiating the Form of the Apple can any object be an apple. Many philosophers since Plato, in ancient, medieval, and modern times, have held similar views: there is a property of being an apple, which all actual apples instantiate.

The property, in this way of thinking, is a *universal*, in that it is present simultaneously in numerous different objects. The opposite of a universal is a *particular*, which is just an ordinary object that is not present in different places at the same time; but the theory that is relevant to us holds that properties are universals.

Theories along these lines have been invoked to account for various phenomena. One example is the nature of similarity. What is

16

it for two things to be similar? It is for them to instantiate at least one property in common, according to this view. Most notably for our present purposes, this kind of theory has been appealed to by Plato and many successors in order to explain the meaning of what are called *general terms*. A general term is a word that is applicable to more than one thing, like *apple, runs, wise, icy*, and other nouns, verbs, and adjectives. The idea is that general terms stand for properties.

Properties are often paired with *relations*. Relations, according to the relevant theories, are also universals, but instead of being instantiated by just one object, wherever they are present, they are supposed to hold between two or more objects. Seeing, for example, might be a relation; it holds between the seer and the seen, and would be the referent of the verb *see* according to the referential theory of meaning. We will see this idea spelt out in Chapter 6.

A neat formal way of summing up the foregoing ideas on meaning that is quite popular in the philosophical literature is the *Russellian proposition*, invented at the beginning of the Twentieth Century by the philosopher Bertrand Russell (1872–1970), one of the founders of analytic philosophy. A *proposition* is the meaning of a declarative sentence. Russell would have claimed that the meaning of the simple declarative sentence *Elizabeth II is wise* was the ordered pair ⟨Elizabeth II, wisdom⟩. The notion of an *ordered pair*, indicated by *angle brackets* (⟨...⟩), derives from set theory; an ordered pair is a set of two things that has a first member and a second member. The first member in this example is Elizabeth II (the monarch, not the name) and the second member is wisdom, or the property of being wise. A sentence whose meaning is a simple Russellian proposition like this would be true if and only if the first member of the proposition has or instantiates the second member.

Since set theory will recur in this book, here is a brief reintroduction to it for those whose schoolroom memories of the subject are hazy. Others can allow their attention to wander freely for the duration of this paragraph. A *set* is a collection of objects. Sets are commonly written by means of curly brackets: the set whose only members are the numbers one and two would be written {1, 2} or {2, 1}. There is no ordering imposed on the members of ordinary sets like this, and the two expressions just written down represent the same set. Things are different with ordered pairs, however, which are the special kinds of sets just described: ⟨1, 2⟩ is not the same set as ⟨2, 1⟩, since the order that the elements appear in is significant. That is enough set theory for now. More will be introduced along the way.

Reference can fruitfully be thought of as the contribution of objects, whether ordinary ones or properties, to Russellian propositions. (By the way, let no-one suspect me of *lèse-majesté* in letting the word *object* be applicable to Elizabeth II—I am using it in the philosophical sense, whereby people are objects too.) The referential theory of meaning arguably has an advantage over the attempt to capture meaning by definitions. To return to our former example, suppose that I have a favourite chair that I call Albert. The sentence *Albert is a chair*, then, would be associated with the Russellian proposition ⟨Albert, chairhood⟩, where *chairhood* is the property of being a chair. (To keep things simple, I am abstracting away from any contributions that might be made by *is* and *a*.) If there really is such a thing as the property of being a chair, it seems that we might have found the meaning of the word *chair* right there, with none of the complicated speculation about leg-count and similar matters that characterized our earlier discussion.

You might be thinking that this sounds a bit too easy. Can we really just decide that one of the ultimate constituents of the world is the property of chairhood and designate this novel entity, with no further ado, as the meaning of the word *chair*? And indeed there is a long and honourable philosophical tradition of scepticism concerning properties, and concerning universals in general. A *realist* concerning universals is someone who accepts their existence, and many eminent philosophers, with Plato at their head, have been realists; but opposed to this camp are the *nominalists*, who believe that there are no such things as universals. This tradition seems to have got under way in the middle ages, with such distinguished exponents as William of Ockham (*c.*1287–1347); and it continues to the present day. William of Ockham, it is good to recall, is the man who gave his name to Ockham's Razor, the maxim that enjoins theory-builders of all kinds not to admit more entities into their theory than is absolutely necessary. Is it really necessary to have our ontological theory accommodate these very bizarre entities that can be in lots of different places at once? Fascinating as the debate is, it would take us too far afield to go into it now; suffice it say that there is no consensus on whether properties of the kind we have been talking about really exist. So they do not obviously provide a firm foundation for the semantics of general terms.

A similar point can be made with regard to proper names, which might perhaps have seemed to constitute an area where the theory performed well. There are lots of proper names, such as *Sherlock Holmes* and *Santa Claus*, that do not name anything that actually exists. But if Santa Claus does not exist, the name *Santa Claus* cannot refer to anything. And yet *Santa Claus* is perfectly meaningful and capable of being used in lots of perfectly innocuous sentences, such as *Santa Claus does not exist*. And so it seems that the referential theory of meaning has run into another problem.

Some advocates of the referential theory, in response to this problem, have seriously proposed that Santa Claus does in fact exist. I assure you that I am not making this up. To be fair to these theorists, they are not claiming that at Christmas we really are liable to have a reindeer-borne, red-clad man crawl down our chimneys. They maintain that Santa Claus is an *abstract object*. In order to assess this claim, we will naturally want to know what abstract objects are supposed to be. But here, perhaps predictably, we encounter further complications.

The difference between abstract and *concrete* objects is widely thought to be of fundamental philosophical significance. All objects are sometimes claimed to fall into one of these two categories. Some paradigm examples of concrete objects are you, me, my computer, the desk at which I am sitting, and my copy of P.G. Wodehouse's *Jeeves and the Feudal Spirit*. Some paradigm examples of abstract objects are numbers, geometrical shapes, and P.G. Wodehouse's *Jeeves and the Feudal Spirit*. (The geometrical shapes of which I speak are the perfect triangles, circles, and so on, studied by mathematicians; and the distinction I am aiming at with the example of the

Jeeves novel is the distinction between the content of a book, which can be manifested in many individual copies, and the individual copies themselves.) The standard conception of abstract objects is that, in contradistinction to concrete objects, they are not located in space or time and do not engage in causal relationships. This makes a certain amount of sense when gauged against the examples I just mentioned. Concrete objects like you and my desk occupy certain locations in space and typically come into and go out of existence. (If you think that there is an eternal afterlife, so that you will never go out of existence, you probably believe, nevertheless, that you came into existence.) The number two, however, and a perfect circle with a radius of exactly 2 cm are not the kinds of things that you will ever pinpoint on a map or trip over on the pavement. (You might see things that approximate to being perfect circles, but it is unlikely in the extreme that you will ever find an absolutely perfect circle in the sublunary world: the circumference of a perfect circle has no width, for one thing.) And, although certain knowledge of these matters may be hard to come by, it seems unlikely that the number two came into existence at a certain point in time or will ever cease to exist. Nor, arguably, can numbers or geometrical shapes cause things to happen.

It is perhaps already evident that works of fiction depart from this standard conception of abstract objects in some ways. In particular, it seems that they come into existence at certain times: they are created by authors. (The alternative is that *Jeeves and the Feudal Spirit* has always existed, at least since the beginning of time, if time had a beginning.) The same thing will presumably apply to fictional characters and characters from folklore: if Jeeves and Sherlock Holmes and Santa Claus are abstract objects, they will presumably be rather unusual ones in that they came into existence at particular times and were created by human beings. But there is nothing to prevent the advocates of the position that Santa Claus exists and is an abstract object from saying that there are different types of abstract object: some, like numbers and geometrical shapes, did not come into existence at particular times, whereas others, such as Santa Claus, did; all, presumably, are not located in space and do not participate in causal relationships in the same way that rocks and desks do.

This theory of fictional characters as abstract objects must be the approximate content of an important part of the referential theory of meaning. What is its status? It turns out to be rather similar to the theory's use of properties. Although many philosophers believe in abstract objects, there are many who do not. The view that there are no abstract objects is, rather confusingly, called *nominalism*. We must distinguish between nominalism about universals, which we saw above, and nominalism about abstract objects; the two are clearly conceptually distinct, and each view can be held consistently without the other. Meanwhile, the view that in fact there are abstract objects is called *platonism*, also rather confusingly. This latter term is rather confusing because it is doubtful that Plato himself was an advocate of platonism in this sense—although his Forms are eternal and are presumably not located in space, they nevertheless have strong causal powers. But these terminological matters aside, why might one be a platonist? Think of numbers, a platonist might reply. If it is true that $2 + 3 = 5$ (and one is hard pressed to deny it), then numbers must exist, for how could this statement about the numbers two, three, and five be true if these numbers do not even exist? But if numbers exist, then we have abstract objects, for surely, as I said above, we are not going to pin down the location of the number two in space or time; nor is there any reason to think that it participates in causal relationships. Why, alternatively, might one be a nominalist about abstract objects? Ockham's Razor, a nominalist will urge, dictates that if we can do without these exceedingly weird entities then we should; and besides, if abstract objects are not spatiotemporally located and do not participate in causal relationships, how do platonists suppose that anyone can acquire knowledge of them? For our acquiring knowledge about something is an event and, by definition, abstract objects do not participate in causing events; so any knowledge that we think we have about abstract objects is either pure confusion or, at best, a dim and confused apprehension of other kinds of objects. This objection, sometimes called the *epistemological argument against platonism*, is a stubborn one. Again, as with the case of nominalism about universals, it would be impracticable to examine in detail all the arguments to be found in this neck of the philosophical woods; suffice it to say that it is by no means obvious that there are any such things as abstract objects, or that we could know about them if there were. It is not clear, then, that it is legitimate to appeal to abstract objects in defence of the referential theory of meaning.

A related concern is the following. The referential theory of meaning says that Santa Claus exists and is an abstract object; furthermore (and this was the point of this metaphysical excursus), the proper name *Santa Claus* is provided by this doctrine with a referent, which it must have if the referential theory of meaning is to be true. So *Santa Claus* refers to a particular existent abstract object. But then the sentence *Santa Claus does not exist* is predicted to say of a particular existent abstract object that it does not exist, which must, of course, be false. But intuitively *Santa Claus does not exist* is true. And this sentence does not seem, intuitively, to be denying the existence of an abstract object; it seems to be denying the existence of a putative concrete object, a jolly, red-clad man who is liable to climb down our chimneys at Christmas. Even if we grant referential theorists the existence of Santa Claus (which is surely about the most generous intellectual concession that one could ever make), problems still abound here. And when the non-existence of Santa Claus poses a problem for your theory, it is time to look for a new theory.

Let us move on, then, to examine the internalist theory. This theory states that word meanings are internal mental structures. The basic idea can also be expressed by saying that meanings are ideas or concepts; or by saying that meanings are in the head. Some version of the theory goes back at least to Aristotle (384–322 BC), who in his treatise *On Interpretation* wrote, 'Spoken words are symbols of mental experiences.' The theory was prominent in the middle ages: the fourteenth-century French philosopher John Buridan, for example, in his *Summulae de dialectica*, declares that 'the capability of speaking was given to us in order that we could signify our concepts to others and also the capacity of hearing was given to us in order that the concepts of speakers could be signified to us.' In the early modern period, a prominent exponent of this view was the English philosopher John Locke (1632–1704). In his *An Essay Concerning*

Human Understanding (1690), Locke wrote, 'words, in their primary or immediate signification, stand for nothing but the ideas in the mind of him that uses them'. And in modern times the view is held by Noam Chomsky and many other linguists and is standard in psychology.

Here is a Chomskyan version of the internalist theory. Language in general, for Chomsky, is basically a psychological phenomenon. Human beings are equipped with certain specialized mental apparatus such as a *mental lexicon*, which contains all the words we know, and a syntactic module, which tells us how to arrange words in grammatical sentences. The whole ensemble of an individual's language-specific mental apparatus is called that person's *language faculty*. Words, according to Chomsky, are mental entities that consist of three parts: phonological information, which tells us how to pronounce them; syntactic information, which tells us what part of speech they are and such things as whether they obligatorily take a direct object (in the case of verbs); and semantic information, or meaning. (In the case of literate people, we can add orthographical information to this list.) The semantic information must be very intricate, since it must give rise to all the phenomena that we noted above when trying to give definitions of words; but it is nearly all inaccessible to consciousness, and details of it can be reconstructed only with painstaking effort, as we have seen. As for the precise form that this semantic information takes, Chomsky has little to say; it is deeply mysterious. (We will see in a short while that contemporary psychologists have tried to flesh out the picture a little.)

Before we go on, it is worth pointing out some consequences of this view. One is that our talk of things like 'the English word *chair*' is misleading. Strictly speaking, according to the internalist view, it is not the case that there is one word *chair*. We should rather say that in your mental lexicon there is a word *chair* with certain phonological, syntactic, and semantic features and in my mental lexicon there is another word *chair* with features that are similar but possibly slightly different. To be clear about this, we should introduce some philosophical terminology about difference. In the case of *numerical difference*, there are two separate objects residing in different places.

In the case of *numerical identity*, we are concerned with exactly one object: we might say that Superman and Clark Kent are (numerically) identical, which boils down to *Superman* and *Clark Kent* being two different names for the same man. Numerical difference (or identity) is to be contrasted with *qualitative difference* (or identity or similarity). Two things could be numerically distinct but qualitatively very similar: two new cars of the same make and colour, for example, would be qualitatively very similar but numerically distinct. The case of the word *chair* in your head and the word *chair* in my head, then, is definitely a case of numerical difference, in that two separate objects are involved; and it may very well be a case of qualitative difference too, in that the chance of our pronouncing these words exactly alike is not very high. (A trained phonetician could almost certainly find some small differences.) It turns out that there is also a good chance that your word *chair* and my word *chair* will differ very slightly in semantic features too, as we will see later. Extrapolating from the case of single words, Chomsky also maintains that there is, strictly speaking, no such thing as English, or French, or Japanese, or any other natural language. If language is purely psychological, and individual speakers' language faculties are the only linguistic things there are, there is no place for any separate object 'English'. There are just lots of groups of human beings with language faculties that resemble each other in sufficient detail for communication to be able to take place; one of these groups we informally call 'English-speakers', another one 'French-speakers', and so on.

So for Chomsky word meanings are parts of words and are all in the head. Now it might seem as if there is an obvious and grave problem with this kind of view, which was pointed out by the English philosopher John Stuart Mill (1806–1873) in his *System of Logic* (1843): 'When I say, "the sun is the cause of day," I do not mean that my idea of the sun causes or excites in me the idea of day; or in other words, that thinking of the sun makes me think of day.' The difficulty is that, if word meanings are just ideas in our heads, it is not obvious how we can use words to talk about things other than ideas in our heads. How do we talk about the outside world? (Note that the referential theory of meaning, whatever may be its flaws, solves this problem in a very immediate way, since word meanings, according to this theory, actually are things in the world.) According to Chomsky, the crucial notion here is *use*: we use words rather like tools to talk about things in the world or focus attention on particular aspects of the world. Responding to the American philosopher Hilary Putnam, who was insisting that there is some relation between speakers, words, and things in the world, Chomsky wrote, 'So there sometimes is . . . , in more or less the sense in which a relation holds of people, hands, and rocks, in that I can use my hand to pick up a rock.' Our usage and understanding of words in this way is spontaneous and unthinking. There must be some deep-seated convention, then, perhaps instigated by biology rather than society, to the effect that when people utter a word whose meaning is a particular internal concept, they are not attempting to draw attention to the concept itself, but rather to things that, as we say, *fall under* that concept.

One advantage of the internalist theory that should already be evident is that it deals much more happily than the referential theory of meaning with terms like *Santa Claus*. Everyone who has heard of Santa Claus presumably has a Santa Claus concept in their heads; they know that nothing, in fact, falls under this concept, but that does not matter. In order to have a meaning for the proper name *Santa Claus*, all we need is the concept.

The internalist theory also deals more readily than the referential theory with another intriguing fact about meaning. In various works, Chomsky has drawn attention to sentences like *Jeeves and the Feudal Spirit is a best-seller and weighs twelve ounces*. What exactly is it that is a best-seller and weighs twelve ounces? I might be tempted to brandish my copy of the book and say, 'This is.' My particular copy might weigh twelve ounces, certainly. But my particular copy cannot be best-selling all by itself: many different copies of a book must sell in order for it to be best-selling. What kind of thing can be best-selling, then? In the light of our previous discussion, the obvious candidate is an abstract object: recall that some philosophers claim that the content of a book is an abstract object that might be realized, as it were, in many concrete copies. So an abstract object might possibly be best-selling, if we follow these philosophers. But an abstract object cannot weigh twelve ounces: since abstract objects are not located in space, they cannot be affected by gravity, which is necessary in order to weigh anything. It seems, then, upon sober reflection, that no actual object can both be a best-seller and weigh twelve ounces. Chomsky sums up the conundrum by saying that the meanings of words of natural languages evidently presuppose the existence of objects that are simultaneously abstract and concrete, which is an impossibility for any actual object. But this presents the referential theory of meaning with a grave difficulty when it comes to finding a referent for the proper name *Jeeves and the Feudal Spirit*, as used in the sentence above: it seems there can be no such object; but the referential theory claims that the meanings of words are objects. The internalist theory, on the other hand, has less of a problem here: it just has to point out what everyone already knows all too well, namely that ideas can be self-contradictory.

This is not to say that there is no problem at all here for the internalist theory of meaning. We still have to explain how it is that we can say something apparently straightforward and true, like the above example, by using self-contradictory concepts. I am not aware of any work on this.

Let us move on to examine the account of word meaning given by contemporary psychology. It seems beyond doubt that normal human beings are equipped with *concepts*. Concepts are mental representations that allow us to classify things we come across and access memorized information about them so that we will know how to behave appropriately towards them. If this object in front of me falls under my concept CHAIR, for example, I know that I can sit on it (unless it also falls under my concept TOY or my concept ART EXHIBIT). If, however, it falls under my concept TIGER, I will not try to sit on it, unless I am possessed of very unusual skills. There is some impressive evidence from experiments on concepts that seems to indicate that the meanings of words (or at least nouns and verbs) are concepts. For example, concepts display a variety of distinctive properties, one of which is *typicality effects*: there seem to be good and less good members of the set of things that fall under a given concept, as diagnosed by how easily experimental subjects can classify them. So if experimental subjects are exposed one at a time to photographs of various objects and instructed to press one button if the object is a bird and a different button if the object is not a bird, with their responses being timed, they will take longer to verify that an emu or a penguin is a bird than they will to verify that a sparrow or a wren is a bird. The idea is that sparrows and wrens in some way correspond more closely to the concept BIRD than emus and penguins do, even though the latter do indeed fall under this concept. Now the point is that in this kind of experiment exactly the same results are obtained whether the stimuli are photographs or words. So if the previous experiment is repeated exactly, with the exception that words and not photographs are flashed up on the screen, subjects will take longer to verify that the words *emu* or *penguin* name birds than they will to verify that the words *sparrow* or *wren* name birds. The logical conclusion is that the same information is being drawn upon each time: there seems to be one concept BIRD, for example, that is accessed no matter whether we are shown a picture of a bird or shown the word for a kind of bird. Since the concept BIRD naturally contains a lot of information about birds it would seem to be a good candidate for the meaning of the word *bird*, and any theory that postulated both the concept BIRD and a separate word-meaning would be seriously uneconomical. Psychologists, therefore, suppose that word meanings are concepts, and that the meanings of complex phrases and sentences are concepts too, derived by combining the constituent concepts.

What theories do psychologists propose about the structure of concepts? There are several theories on offer. For current purposes, it will suffice to examine the best known one—the *prototype theory*. The prototype theory was proposed by the American psychologist Eleanor Rosch in the 1970s. Imagine a concept and some things that fall under it—the concept BIRD and various birds, for example. The prototype theory says that the concept is a summary representation of features that the things in question can have, together with weightings indicating how important it is to have those features in order to fall under the concept. For example, in the case of BIRD, there might be a feature 'feathered' that would be highly weighted, since birds quite generally have feathers. (Not plucked ones, though.) Similarly for features like 'egg-laying', 'winged' and 'capable of flying'. But other features like 'brown' would be less highly weighted. In fact, since birds can be all kinds of different colours, lots of contradictory colour features would be listed, each with fairly low weightings. So what happens if we are presented with an object and asked if it is a bird? Basically, we go through the features in the concept BIRD and add up the weightings of the features that the object has; we might also subtract the weightings of at least some features in the concept that the object does not have. If the final sum exceeds a certain threshold, the *categorization criterion*, we judge that the object falls under the concept—for example, that Tweety is a bird. Otherwise, we judge that the object does not fall under the concept. It can be seen how this theory accounts for the typicality effects that we just noted. In the case of a sparrow or a wren, all of the heavily weighted features ('feathered', 'winged', 'beaked', and so on) are present, and they easily combine to exceed the categorization criterion. But in the case of a penguin, many of these heavily weighted features are not present, or are not obviously present. (Do penguins have feathers? It turns out that they do, but from a distance they look rather like they have fur. And do those flippers count as wings? They certainly do not enable their owners to fly.) So the categorization system is left scrabbling, as it were, to exceed the threshold by means of less heavily weighted features, or by heavily weighted features only belatedly recognized as being applicable.

While its treatment of typicality effects is laudable, the prototype theory is less promising in other arenas. One important example involves *compositionality*. The principle of compositionality states that the meaning of a complex phrase is determined solely by the meanings of its parts and their syntactic arrangement. Some principle of this sort seems necessary because of the *productivity* of language: we can produce and understand an indefinitely large number of novel phrases whose meanings cannot be listed separately (phrase by phrase) in our mental lexicons. So, for example, you understand me if I write about *a winged chihuahua, Santa Claus on a Harley Davidson,* and *a dramatic reading of the telephone directory,* even if (as is likely) you have never heard or read those phrases before. We must be able to take the words out of which these novel phrases are constructed and combine their meanings somehow in order to arrive at the meaning of the whole. It has been alleged by the American philosopher Jerry Fodor that the prototype theory fails to account for compositionality in a range of basic cases. Take the phrase *pet fish*, for example. Its meaning, according to the prototype theory, must be a concept of the kind described above. So it must give heavy weighting to features that pet fish generally have, such as 'brightly coloured', 'small', and 'lives in bowls or small tanks'. But it is hard to see how a concept with these features can be the result of combining the concepts attached to the words *pet* and *fish*: neither pets in general nor fish in general are brightly coloured, small, or dwellers in bowls or tanks. So the meaning that the prototype theory would give to *pet fish* cannot be derived systematically from the meanings that this theory would give to *pet* and *fish*. This is generally seen as a bad thing.

There are other theories of concepts in psychology, but they are subject to other problems. This is not to counsel despair. A tremendous amount of progress has been made in the psychology of concepts since the 1970s. The discovery of typicality effects, for example, is a major landmark that must be accounted for by any theory in this area. And for our current purposes, we do not need to profess allegiance to any particular theory of concepts in order to hold the view that word meanings are concepts, if by that we just mean that word meanings are internal mental structures.

One objection that seemingly threatens every internalist theory of word meaning focuses on the apparent possibility of accurate communication. This objection goes back at least to the great German philosopher Gottlob Frege (1848–1925), the founder of modern logic and analytic philosophy. If word meanings are internal mental structures, then it is entirely possible that you and I have different meanings attached to what we ordinarily take to be the same word. Take the word *jejune*, for example, whose traditional definition is something like 'meagre, unsatisfying'. In one sense, of course, the internalist theory is explicitly committed to the meanings that we attribute to *jejune* being different: they are numerically distinct objects. Now

Frege and many philosophers since have seen sinister implications in the idea that a word has lots of numerically distinct meanings, a different one in the head of every person who knows it. For what could guarantee that these numerically distinct meanings would be qualitatively identical? And if the numerically distinct meanings are not qualitatively identical, then it seems that grave breakdowns of communication could ensue. You would mean one thing by *jejune* and I would mean something significantly different. We would be talking past each other.

It is certainly true that there is an impressive amount of qualitative similarity between the meanings that people seem to assume for a given word; and it is true that linguistic communication often proceeds quite well. But it is far from clear that we need to fall back on the referential theory of meaning in order to ensure this. The trouble is that the referential theory, even though it says that meanings themselves are things in the world, must provide some account of how people get to know about these things; for people must have mental representations of word meanings in order to function linguistically, even if word meanings are not mental representations. What would the meaning of the word *jejune* be according the referential theory? Presumably it would be the property of jejuneness. Now how likely is it that people will be able to get a clear idea of that property? And how likely is it that everyone will converge on exactly the same idea? Our previous discussions come back into play here. To start with, some philosophers believe that properties are abstract objects. But that, as we have seen, runs the risk of making them immune from any means we might have of gaining knowledge about them. What about the other option, which is to say that jejuneness is a universal and a concrete object? Then it has to be an extremely strange concrete object that is present in a spatially disconnected fashion in everything that is jejune. How likely are people to gain a good idea of something as complicated as the universal of jejuneness? And with what senses or mental faculties do they do so? It is entirely unclear how this is supposed to work. It is somewhat mysterious, then, how appealing to the referential theory of meaning is supposed to help us at this point.

Furthermore, when we come to examine the alleged interpersonal identity of meaning that the referential view is supposed to guarantee, and the internalist view imperil, it turns out to be a chimera. To start with *jejune*, many people who know this word associate it with a meaning something like 'puerile', as if it were related to French *jeune* 'young'; it is occasionally even spelled *jejeune*. Others, as I mentioned, associate it with a meaning 'meagre, unsatisfying', which is derived from that of the ancestor of the word, Latin *jejunus* 'fasting'; people who use this meaning of the word are likely to castigate the 'puerile' meaning as a malapropism, but it cannot be denied that both meanings exist, in the internalist sense. So here is a first example of lack of interpersonal identity of meaning. And we do not need to search out relatively rare words like *jejune* to make this point. The psychological literature reveals substantial speaker variation even in the case of common words. In a classic 1978 paper, the Princeton psychologists Michael McCloskey and Sam Glucksberg tested thirty Princeton undergraduates twice, in sessions one month apart, on whether they thought that items designated by given words were members of categories indicated by further words. Subjects were shown pairs of words like *handkerchief–clothing*, for example, and asked to indicate whether things that could be described by the first word could also be described by the second. It was found that 45% of responses indicated that a handkerchief was an item of clothing, while 55% indicated that it was not. This indicates quite substantial disagreement over the meaning of *clothing, handkerchief,* or both. In other findings, 30% of responses indicated that curtains were furniture, while 70% did not; 47% of responses claimed that lobsters were fish, while 53% did not; and, rather alarmingly, it was averred 35% of the time that poets were not animals. You may be relieved to know that women were claimed to lie outside the animal kingdom only 3% of the time. As if this were not enough to subvert the doctrine of interpersonal identity of meaning, the psychologists found that substantial numbers of subjects actually changed the answers they gave between the two sessions. Ten undergraduates changed their minds over the course of the month on whether curtains were furniture, for example; and two had second thoughts on the question of whether women were animals. (It is unfortunately not recorded which aspect of Princeton life it was that prompted these students to reconsider.) So far are we from the alleged interpersonal identity of meaning that we even have to deal with breakdowns of intrapersonal identity of meaning.

It is time to bring this discussion of the referential and internalist theories of word meaning to a close, at least temporarily. The reader will doubtless have noted my own sympathies for the internalist camp; but I cannot stress too strongly that in this introductory treatment I have tried only to give a flavour of the debate. I have not tried to cover every argument that has been made on this topic; and many philosophers and linguists far more venerable and learned than I am are convinced of the referentialist conclusion.

3

Semantic properties of words

In this chapter I will discuss some semantic properties that words are traditionally supposed to have. I will concentrate on synonymy, ambiguity, and vagueness.

With all the fine variation in the meanings that different people attribute to what we loosely call the same word, you may be wondering whether two different words ever have the same meaning. In other words, you might be wondering about the status of *synonymy*. For two words to be synonymous, traditionally speaking, is for them to have the same meaning. In internalist terms, we would recognize two ways in which this might happen: the meanings that the two words had could be numerically identical or merely qualitatively identical. The first possibility would be realized if one concept in someone's head was simultaneously part of two different words. The second possibility would be realized if two words, whether in one head or in different ones, had qualitatively identical meanings.

But do any synonymous pairs of words really exist? As soon as one starts looking into fine shades of meaning, it might appear doubtful. For example, a patient might lie on a psychoanalyst's *couch* with perfect propriety; but if they were to lie on the same person's *sofa*, we might suspect a breach of professional ethics, since the latter furnishing would probably be in the psychoanalyst's home. Similarly, having a *big* brother has chronological implications that having a *large* brother does not—to say nothing of the possible totalitarian overtones. But one can push scepticism about synonymy too far. It is sometimes claimed, for example, that pairs of words like *napkin* and *serviette* (or *pudding* and *dessert*) have different meanings merely because they are used by different social classes—the Mitfordesque distinction between U and non-U vocabulary. But I have yet to be convinced. It seems more satisfactory to say that the members of these pairs have the same meaning and that knowledge of their social overtones is knowledge of a different type. (That is, we might have to add a set of sociolinguistic features to the phonological, syntactic, semantic, and orthographical ones that make up each word.) I cannot think of any cunning science-fiction scenario in which napkins are not serviettes or vice versa; so, as far as I can tell, the intensions of the two words are the same. This is strong evidence that their meanings are the same. And finally I cannot detect any difference in meaning between *gorse* and *furze*. Lack of difference here is especially likely because people often grow up knowing only one of these words and learn the second one late in life, on the basis of the one they already know. The learning process goes something like, 'Aha! *Furze* is evidently another word for *gorse*.' I think, then, that we should not be unwilling to admit synonymy into our semantic theories.

That leaves ambiguity and vagueness. These two properties are commonly dealt with in tandem, because, while it is often possible to see that a word is either ambiguous or vague, it is sometimes difficult to tell which. A word is ambiguous if it has more than one meaning. A word is vague (in the currently relevant sense) if it has a meaning that does not distinguish between two or more different kinds of thing. The word *chair*, for example, is ambiguous between (at least) an indefinable device that may have something to do with sitting, a person in charge of a committee, and a university professorship. When I was talking about chairs earlier, I was tacitly ignoring the other meanings, and you probably went along with this simplification with nary a qualm—we are good at screening out irrelevant meanings. The word *horse*, on the other hand, is vague in that it does not specify whether we are talking about a racehorse, a carthorse, or a charger. Or at least so I suppose. One could possibly maintain that *horse* is ambiguous between these various meanings; but here that hypothesis seems a bit far-fetched because of the ease with which we can perceive (although not describe) a common element, horsiness, in all these cases. Having said that, however, we should complicate things by admitting that *horse* is both vague and ambiguous: as well

34

as the familiar quadruped, it can also designate heroin and, among other things, various complicated ropes on sailing ships whose functions are largely impenetrable. Many words, in fact, are both ambiguous and vague, in that they have more than one meaning and at least one of these meanings applies equally well to various kinds of things. *Blue* is such an example: one could be depressed, navy blue, and sky blue, although hopefully not all at once.

A somewhat trickier case is a word like *column*. We talk about columns in architecture, gossip columns, and columns of soldiers marching into battle. Here it is tempting to see different meanings (how could Trajan's Column be the same kind of thing as a description of the latest excesses of some starlet?); but it is also tempting to see important commonality. In historical terms, it is likely that newspaper columns and military columns were so-named because they shared the shape of Ionic columns and the like; and this relationship is still perceptible. So should we say that *column* has one basic meaning, having to do with shape, and that it is vague as between various things of this form? Or should we say that the basic meaning is the architectural one and that the others are metaphorical extensions (whatever *they* are) based on shared shape? Or should we alternatively say that at least some of these uses have crystallized into separate meanings, making the word ambiguous? It is not a straightforward matter. But we can obtain some insight, once more, by means of a warped counterfactual scenario. Imagine that some newspapers started printing the effusions of their columnists in perfectly square blocks of type, or even circular ones. Would we still use the word *column* to describe these pieces? I think we would; and although I can well imagine that some people would start referring to 'newspaper squares' and 'newspaper circles', I think this would rather be a poor attempt at humour than a serious semantic objection. This indicates that in my mental lexicon, at least, the journalistic sense of the word is distinct from the architectural one.

I will shortly distinguish between two kinds of ambiguity, but first I should say a little more about the term *vague*: *vague* is ambiguous. The usage of *vague* that I just described is common among linguists but not among philosophers. Philosophers refer to the kind of vagueness just outlined as *generality*. They reserve the term *vague* for words that seem to give rise to borderline cases: objects that do not clearly fall under a predicate and do not clearly not fall under it either. For example, suppose that a man becomes completely bald, not all at once, but by a gradual and debilitating process whereby a few hairs at a time are lost. At the start of the process, he has a full head of hair, and is thus clearly not bald. At the end of it, he has no hair whatsoever on his head, and so is clearly bald. Just before the end of the process, when he has only two or three hairs remaining on his head, he is pretty clearly bald. Or at least we would have no compunction about saying so. But what about a man who has 100 hairs on his head, evenly distributed? Or one who has 500? There comes a point when one feels uncomfortable in saying either that the man in question is bald, or that he is not bald. He is a borderline case, and the word *bald* is thereby shown to be vague. This meaning of *vague* is clearly distinct from the first one described, in that one could imagine a word meaning with the following properties: several different kinds of things fall under it (making it vague in the first sense), but its external boundaries are completely sharp (making it not vague in the second sense). I am not sure if any actual word meanings are like that, however: the 'colour' meaning of *blue* is surely not, since although it encompasses both navy blue and sky blue it also shades off very gradually into purple. The 'equine quadruped' meaning of *horse* is a better candidate, but even here I suspect it is possible to find borderline cases by travelling back along the evolutionary line that led to modern horses, insofar as it can be reconstructed. Was the relatively recent Plesippus a horse? It certainly looks like one in modern reconstructions. What if we go back all the way to Hyracotherium (or Eohippus), which was about two feet long and looked nothing like a horse? At some point along the line we are likely to find an animal that is neither clearly a horse nor clearly not a horse. Vagueness, in this sense as in the other, afflicts a huge proportion of natural language words.

The two kinds of ambiguity I mentioned above are *polysemy* and *homonymy*. Polysemy is the state of affairs whereby one word has many meanings, where a word is to be understood, as previously, as a collection of phonological, syntactic, and semantic features. (It is not necessary to buy into Chomskyan internalism to make this distinction, though; all these collections and features could be abstract objects, or indeed objects lying in a field somewhere, for current purposes.) The idea is that some collections of this kind contain one set of phonological features linked with one set of syntactic features linked with two or more sets of semantic features. The whole (or its representation) forms just one entry in the mental lexicon—one *lexical entry*, as we say. The different meanings of a polysemous word are called *senses* of that word. This picture is to be contrasted with homonymy, which involves not one but two (or more) lexical entries. So in the case of homonymy there are two distinct words, with different meanings, that happen to be pronounced the same. A distinction is sometimes made between homonymy in a narrower sense, which requires the two words to have not only the same pronunciation but also the same spelling, and *homophony*, which requires only the same pronunciation; but researchers often do not bother with this, since writing is so obviously a late and secondary addition to human linguistic ability, and to this day many languages do not have a written form.

Why has this distinction been posited? The traditional justification was really no more than an intuition that some relevant meanings were much more closely related to each other than others. The classic example of homonymy is *bank* and *bank*, where one of those items is to be understood as a pleasant word designating the sides of rivers, and the other one is an unpleasant word having to do with subprime loans. Not much semantic overlap there, one would think. On the other hand, the architectural, journalistic, and military meanings of *column* are generally reckoned to be different senses of one polysemous word. We already noted their obvious semantic relatedness. These judgements are reflected in dictionaries, which without exception, as far as I know, have two separate entries or headwords for *bank* and *bank* and just one entry with lots of subdivisions for *column*. The idea is that our mental lexicons reproduce the structure of our paper lexicons in this respect. But it must be admitted that the grounds on which this distinction was made were less solid than we would like: there is no evident reason why intuitions that purport to be about complex internal mental structure (or epistemically inaccessible abstract objects) should be trusted. Certainly the history of the words in question is no help. The various senses of *column* are, of course, historically related; but so, unfortunately, are *bank* and *bank*. The *OED*, in its entry for the financial *bank*, records that the earliest meaning of this word was 'money-dealer's table'; this derived from French *banque*, which in turn was based on Italian *banca*, which had the same meaning, and which was a loanword from a Germanic language, the whole ultimately deriving from a Proto-Germanic root *bank- meaning 'shelf, bench'. (Proto-Germanic is the name given to the hypothesized language from which all the Germanic languages, such as English, German, and Dutch, descended; an asterisk before a word in historical linguistics means that the word is not directly attested in any source but is reconstructed by scholars.) The same root also gave English *bank* in the topological sense, originally a 'shelf' of land. From an examination of the traditional distinction between polysemy and homonymy, then, it is unclear whether we should really posit both. In particular, there is an alternative hypothesis according to which separate senses of allegedly polysemous words are really just separate words, with their own lexical entries in the mental lexicon: polysemy is really homonymy, in short.

Fortunately, light has been shed on this issue by brain imaging. The argument here is rather complex, but the end result will be worth it. In an ingenious experiment published in 2006, the neuroscientists Liina Pylkkänen, Rodolfo Llinás, and Gregory Murphy, all of New York University, used magnetoencephalography to scrutinize the brain-activity of seventeen subjects as they read and responded to phrases involving homonymous and polysemous words. Magnetoencephalography (MEG) is a technique that measures the magnetic fields generated by electric currents in the brain. Brain activity involves neurons transmitting tiny electric currents to other cells via synapses; so by measuring the different strengths and locations of magnetic fields around the head as a mental task is performed, researchers can sometimes gain a fair idea of when and where various mental events take place. The crucial MEG measurement used by

Pylkkänen and her colleagues is called the *M350*: a surge of magnetic amplitude that takes place in the left temporal cortex (of a right-handed subject) between 300 and 400 milliseconds (msec) after the visual presentation of a word. (The temporal cortex is the outer part of the brain near the ear.) Previous research, which I will not try to summarize, had shown convincingly that the M350 was a sign of *lexical activation*, or the successful location in one's mental lexicon of a word that one is presented with. One crucial fact to note is that the M350 does not always take place at exactly the same time for any given person; the timing, or *latency*, is subject to several factors and can be manipulated.

Pylkkänen and her colleagues used three findings about varying M350 latencies to argue for their conclusion about polysemy and homonymy. They had their subjects look at words on a screen while their M350 latencies were measured; that is, while it was measured how long they took to find each word in their mental lexicons. One type of stimulus involved words that would traditionally be classed as homonyms. For example, subjects saw the words *river* and *bank* flash up on the screen separately but with only a 300 msec gap between them; they were expecting a two-word phrase and had been told to interpret the words in this fashion. After a longer pause, another two word phrase would be flashed up in the same way. The next one might be *savings bank*, a phrase that clearly uses the homonym of the noun that featured in the first phrase. On average, subjects took 355 msec to locate the second homonym in their mental lexicons on trials like this. (Many different pairs of homonyms were used, of course—not just *bank* and *bank*.) But when one of the homonym-containing phrases like *savings bank* was preceded by an unrelated control phrase, like *salty dish*, the subjects took only 334 msec, on average, to look up the homonym. So if you have to find a word in your mental lexicon, you are slowed down if you have just seen a homonym of it—it is as if your processing faculties are confused by having seen something phonologically similar that is not in fact the word they are after. This is the first finding about M350 latencies. A second type of stimulus used nouns that were semantically related but not phonologically similar. So the subjects might see *lined paper* flash up on the screen, followed by *monthly magazine*: *paper* and *magazine* are semantically related, in that one meaning of *paper* and one meaning of *magazine* apply to similar kinds of things. The M350 latencies for the second noun in trials of this type averaged out at 345 msec. This is to be compared to trials in which phrases like the second one just mentioned, *monthly magazine*, were preceded by unrelated controls, like *clock tick*. The average M350 latency in these trials was a considerably higher 367 msec. So if you have to find a word in your mental lexicon, you are speeded up if you have just seen a semantically related (but phonologically unrelated) word. This is the second finding about M350 latencies.

Slower processing caused by phonological similarity is called *phonological inhibition*. Faster processing caused by semantic similarity is called *semantic priming*. We can sum up the first two findings as phonological inhibition and semantic priming.

We can now do some reasoning about the two hypotheses that we started with, namely that polysemy and homonymy work as traditionally imagined, and that alleged polysemy actually works just like homonymy. Let us take the allegedly polysemous word *paper*, which can be used to refer to a kind of physical material made from wood pulp or to a newspaper, including the content, political bias, and bureaucratic structure of a newspaper. (It would be possible to say, 'That boring, liberal paper just fired its best writers. It's not worth the paper it's printed on.' The first sentence here sounds like another Chomskyan example of natural language meanings presupposing the existence of impossible objects.) If *paper* in the sense of 'material made from wood pulp' and *paper* in the sense of 'newspaper' are in fact two separate lexical entries, contrary to the traditional polysemy hypothesis, then they would be rather like a combination of normal homonyms, on the one hand, and semantically related words, on the other. They would be like regular homonyms in that their pronunciation would be identical while their meanings were different. But their meanings would be semantically related to an extent not found in regular homonyms, and in this respect they would be like the pairs of semantically related nouns (*paper–magazine*) that featured in the second kind of stimulus described above. So what effect would we predict on the M350 latencies if we followed *lined paper* with *liberal paper*, where the two occurrences of *paper* evidently have the two different interpretations in question? How, that is, would the M350 latency for the second occurrence of *paper* in this condition compare to the M350 latency that *paper* in *lined paper* would have when preceded by an unrelated control? The prediction seems to be that there would be little or no difference between the latencies in the two conditions: phonological inhibition would tend to make the last latency in *lined paper–liberal paper* longer than normal (by about 20 msec); but semantic priming would tend to make the last latency in this condition shorter than normal (by about 20 msec). So the two effects should cancel each other out. On the other hand, the traditional polysemy hypothesis predicts that the last latency will be shorter than normal. It is unclear whether we should expect seman-tic priming to occur between the senses of one polysemous word, since the semantic priming effect was established using semantically related distinct words; but there is another well established effect called *repetition priming*, which says that latencies will be reduced in processing a word when one has just been exposed to the very same word a short time before. Now the crucial difference between the two hypotheses about polysemy is that one, the traditional one, says that just one word is in play in these cases, while the other hypothesis says that two or more separate words are involved. So the traditional hypothesis but not its upstart challenger predicts shorter latencies due to repetition priming, if nothing else.

So what happened when Pylkkänen and her colleagues exposed their subjects to trials like *lined paper–liberal paper*? The answer is that the M350 latencies for the second occurrence of *paper* aver-aged out at 337 msec. And when *liberal paper* was preceded by an unrelated control? The average latency was a considerably longer 361 msec. So the prediction of the traditional polysemy hypothesis is rather impressively borne out.

Given that we can apparently resolve a question about word mean-ing by measuring small magnetic fields near people's ears, you might be tempted to suppose that the internalist view of meaning is thereby bolstered and the referentialist one consigned to irrelevance. There is something to be said for this view. And it should be added that the research just described is merely a drop in, if not an ocean, then at least a respectably sized sea of knowledge about the location and timing of linguistic processes within the brain. But things are not quite so simple. Philosophers who hold the referential view of meaning would not, presumably, deny that the objects that are word meanings have representations in the brain, in virtue of which we know about them—our mental representation of the universal of jejuneness, for example. So they would presumably interpret the experiment just described as giving us information about the structure of our mental representations of word meanings; it would not, on this view, give us information about word meanings themselves. This is all perfectly coherent. But once more Ockham's Razor looms large: it looks like the referentialists have to posit all the linguistically-relevant mental structure that the internalists posit, and then a whole set of separate word meanings on top of that. So the number of entities they posit is vastly larger than the number posited by the internalists. So the pressure to make do with the more parsimonious internalist theory is immense.

4

What are sentence meanings?

The debate between the referential and internalist theories of meaning continues, albeit in slightly modified form, when we turn our attention to sentences.

The internalist theory of meaning maintains that the meanings of sentences are internal mental structures, just as the meanings of words are. The difference is that these mental structures will be more complex than word meanings. Indeed they must presumably be at least partly composed out of word meanings. Recall our discussion of compositionality: in order to account for the fact that we can produce and understand an apparently unlimited number of phrases, we think that the meaning of a complex phrase is arrived at systematically on the basis of the meanings of the words that compose it, plus their syntactic arrangement. (Why do we mention syntax? *Man bites dog* differs in meaning from *Dog bites man*, even though they contain the same words.) This principle naturally holds just as well for sentences as it does for any other kind of phrase. So according to the internalist theory, the meaning of a sentence is an internal mental structure arrived at in a compositional fashion from the meanings of the words in the sentence and their syntactic arrangement. Beyond this minimal picture it is difficult to go. As we have seen with the example of the prototype theory of concepts and the pet fish, giving any account of the nature of these mental structures is a tricky business in the extreme. I will shortly be mentioning some simple mathematical models that might be insightful, however.

The referential theory of meaning maintained that the meanings of many words were objects in the world—particular people, chairs, properties, and so on. But it can hardly do the same with sentence meanings. It is plausible on the face of it that the sole semantic contribution of *Elizabeth II* is Elizabeth II. But one cannot stroll up to Buckingham Palace and find the meaning of *Elizabeth II is wise* playing with the corgis. What to do? Referentialists generally suppose that sentence meanings are abstract objects. Indeed we saw an example of this in Chapter 2: the meaning of *Elizabeth II is wise* is sometimes claimed to be the Russellian proposition ⟨Elizabeth II, wisdom⟩. Recall that the angle brackets just denote an ordered pair, which is a kind of set. Now sets, although I did not stress the point before, are abstract objects. Even if their members are spatiotemporally located, the sets themselves are not, according to the standard conception of them. We will shortly see another kind of set that sentence meanings have been claimed to be. But first we should study the motivations for the basic claim that sentence meanings are abstract objects.

Part of the reason that many philosophers like this position is to be found in concerns about communication. If there is one object that is the meaning of an uttered sentence, this seems to provide a better foundation for successful communication than the situation that the internalist alternative would envisage, namely numerically different meanings in the heads of the speaker and hearer. We looked at this argument in Chapter 2, where we noted that perfectly shared meaning is perhaps rarer than these philosophers like to think.

But there are also independent arguments for the position that sentence meanings, in particular, are abstract objects. Here is one which has been offered by the American philosopher Stephen Schiffer and which interacts in interesting ways with ideas that we have already met. Consider the sentence *Harold believes that there is life on Venus, and so does Fiona.* From this, Schiffer urges, we can validly deduce the truth of a second sentence, *There is something they both believe—to wit, that there is life on Venus,* where *they,* of course, is to be taken as referring to Harold and Fiona. Why does the truth of the second sentence follow from the truth of the first? Schiffer suggests that the most straightforward way of accounting for this is to take the sentences at face value, as he puts it. That is to say that we should be guided by the syntax of the sentences and a very simple semantics for them. Unpacking the elliptical example used by Schiffer (. . . *and so does Fiona*), we start out with two sentences: *Harold believes that there is life on Venus* and *Fiona believes that there is life on Venus*. They are obviously identical except for their subjects; and they both appear to be of the form Subject-Verb-Object, with the *that*-clause being considered as a complex kind of object. Giving a semantics for these sentences of the kind that we have seen, Schiffer proposes that these sentences state, of Harold and Fiona respectively, that they stand in a particular relation, the belief relation, to a particular object, the proposition that there is life on Venus. If that is so, we then have a very simple explanation of the intuition that *There is something they both believe* follows from these statements. The situation would be exactly parallel to saying that Harold sees Esmerelda and Fiona sees Esmerelda and concluding that there is someone they both see. What kind of thing could the proposition that there is life on Venus be, if Fiona and Harold both stand in the belief relation to it? Here we follow some steps that are by now familiar. If there is one object to which each of these people stand in the belief relation, it cannot be something that is hidden, as it were, inside the head of one of them. It must be publicly accessible. But it cannot be a concrete object. The proposition that there is life on Venus is surely not located anywhere in space, not even on Venus. So it must be an abstract object.

So the argument, in summary, goes as follows: here is a fact about language, that *There is something they both believe* follows from *Harold believes that there is life on Venus and so does Fiona*; this fact receives its most straightforward explanation if we accept that the *that*-clause refers to something, namely the proposition that there is life on Venus; and the proposition that there is life on Venus cannot be a concrete object and therefore must be an abstract object.

It is open to an internalist to reply, however, that *There is something they both believe* is ambiguous. On Schiffer's way of reading it, the sentence does indeed assert the existence of an object to which both Harold and Fiona stand in the belief relation. An internalist will say that on that reading the sentence is simply false and in no way follows from *Harold believes that there is life on Venus and so does Fiona*. On another reading, the sentence would not be claiming anything so ontologically drastic. It would be claiming something milder, perhaps that Harold's belief and Fiona's belief are qualitatively identical. We can compare a sentence like *There is something they both own*. This could mean that there is a particular concrete object of which Harold and Fiona are joint owners; but alternatively it could mean that there is a kind of object such that Harold and Fiona both own objects of that kind. To an assertion that Harold and Fiona's possessions are completely dissimilar, it would be possible to reply, 'No, there is something they both own—a house'. This would not necessarily imply that they own the same house. The internalist can reply to Schiffer's argument, then, by saying that it is only on the harmless second reading that *There is something they both believe* follows from *Harold believes that there is life on Venus and so does Fiona*; no far-reaching metaphysical conclusions can be drawn from this fact.

Of course the theory that sentence meanings are abstract objects also suffers from the epistemological objection to abstract objects that we examined in the last chapter. Since abstract objects are supposed to be causally isolated from creatures like us, there is no evident way in which we could know about them even if they did exist.

Even though the theory that sentence meanings are abstract objects faces difficulties, it is still worth contemplating the two main kinds of abstract object that they have been claimed to be. The reason is that these two kinds of abstract object are mathematical objects, and it might very well be possible to use objects of this kind as mathematical models of internal mental structures. For example, the first kind of abstract object is one we have already seen: Russellian propositions. The idea I have in mind is that one could keep pieces of notation like ⟨Elizabeth II, wisdom⟩ and interpret them not as denoting abstract objects but as showing us something about the structure of the relevant internal mental structures. In this case, presumably, the mathematical model would be telling us that the meaning of

Elizabeth II is wise would be a pairing of the speaker's concept of Elizabeth II with the speaker's concept of wisdom. The basic idea is not very radical, even though it involves a significant reinterpretation of the notation. We are already familiar with what the physicist Eugene Wigner (1902–1995) called 'the unreasonable effectiveness of mathematics in the natural sciences': theories in physics, chemistry, biology, and other areas already use mathematics very successfully to show the structure of the concrete world. Why should the same not be done by semanticists who are sympathetic to the internalist picture of meaning? Meanings on this view, after all, are just part of our heads.

The second kind of abstract object that sentence meanings have been claimed to be is sets of *possible worlds*. We will eventually see an unexpected empirical pay-off from this conception. But first it is appropriate to examine some of the background to this strange idea.

A possible world is something like an alternative universe. (But the actual universe counts as possible too, of course.) These mysterious entities are often invoked by philosophers and linguists to elucidate notions of *modality*: things such as possibility, necessity, and contingency. The idea arguably originates with John Duns Scotus ('the Scot', d.1308), 'the Subtle Doctor', one of the greatest (and most difficult) medieval philosophers, in his theory of contingency. A *contingent* event, roughly speaking, is supposed to be able to happen or not. It is distinguished from an event or state of affairs that is *necessary*, which could not have turned out otherwise. I am sitting down now. But I could have been standing up (or so I like to think). So my sitting now is contingent. But two plus three just has to equal five; mathematical truths are widely supposed to be necessary. Now what does the world have to be like, asks Scotus, for us to be able to say quite truly (or so we like to think) that now, at this very moment when I am sitting down, I could have been standing up? His theory distinguishes *moments of time* from what he calls *moments of nature*, which are something like possibilities: corresponding to this one moment of time are at least two moments of nature, in at least one of which I am standing up. Or, as devotees of science fiction would say, there is an alternative universe in which I am standing up right now. Or, as philosophers would say, there is a possible world in which I am standing now. Scotus used the idea to draw comforting conclusions about the freedom of the will. When I seem to be faced with a choice between two courses of action, I really do have a choice, according to Scotus: there are different moments of nature in which I do different things. I am not just proceeding along a path preordained.

But it is the use of possible worlds by the great philosopher and mathematician Gottfried Wilhelm Leibniz (1646–1716) that is perhaps best known. Leibniz was a polymathic genius, who, among other achievements, was the co-discoverer of calculus (with Isaac Newton). But possible worlds enter his thought in a very different area, and arguably a less successful one: his response to the problem of evil. The *problem of evil* faces all religions (like Judaism and Christianity) that believe that God is omniscient, omnipotent, and benevolent. It points to the huge amount of suffering in the world, suffering caused not only by human beings (whose exercise of free will might be thought to be a counterbalancing good) but also by such impersonal phenomena as earthquakes, famine, and disease. If God were omniscient, He would know about all this suffering; if He were omnipotent, He would be able to put a stop to it; and He if were benevolent, He would want to. But suffering exists. Therefore there can be no omniscient, omnipotent, and benevolent God. So, at least, says the advocate of the problem of evil. In response, Leibniz claims that the actual world is the best of all possible worlds. God, being benevolent, would have created no other. It is not clear exactly what constraints he thought impinged upon possible worlds in such a way that there could not be a better one than ours. But he points out that not all things that are possible individually can possibly exist together, and so absolute perfection in all things might not be possible: the best of all possible worlds is the one in which good most definitively outweighs evil. And he also cautions that the happiness of human beings might not have been the only criterion by which God judged the goodness of the possible worlds he contemplated. Not surprisingly, this response has not met with widespread approbation. The French Enlightenment *philosophe* Voltaire (1694–1778) attacked it in perhaps the most telling way, by satire: the eponymous hero of his novel *Candide, ou l'Optimisme* (1759) enthusiastically soaks up the Leibnizian doctrines of his tutor Pangloss; after Candide becomes an adherent of the view that this is the best of all possible worlds, a series of magnificently appalling things befalls him, the amusing narration of which occupies much of the rest of the book. *Optimism*, by the way, is the name of Leibniz's theological system; but it is not clear that *Pessimism* would not be a better word for it: as Candide says while being spanked to music by the Inquisition in the midst of the Lisbon earthquake of 1755, if this is the best of all possible worlds, what are the others like?

It is time to say a bit more about what exactly possible worlds are supposed to be; we will then be in a position to assess their use in semantics. There have been various views on this. Leibniz evidently thought that possible worlds were nothing more than possibilities entertained in the mind of God: in a letter to the theologian and philosopher Antoine Arnauld (1612–1694) from 14 July 1686, he says, 'there exists no other reality in purely possible things than the one they possess in the divine understanding.' The idea is that God contemplated all possible worlds before deciding which one to create.

A prominent modern alternative, espoused by the late Princeton philosopher David Lewis (1941–2001), is called *modal realism*: other possible worlds exist in exactly the same way that the actual world does. A world, according to Lewis, is 'a maximal mereological sum of spatiotemporally interrelated things'. In other words, a world is something each of whose parts is related in space and time to all of its other parts, and which is such that there is no spatially or temporally more extensive thing that has *it* as a part. There is no spatial path or temporal succession between different Lewisian worlds, then; each of them is an island, as it were, inaccessible from all the others. What we call the *actual* world is just the world where we happen to live; if there are other people in other worlds who speak a language much like English, they can with equal justification use the word *actual* about their own world. The word *actual*, in Lewis's view, is an *indexical*; that is to say that it is a word like *I* or *here* which is used to refer to different things by different speakers at different places. Lewis's theory is apt to provoke what he called 'the incredulous stare', although he maintained that incredulous stares outnumbered reasoned objections in response to it. Not everyone dealing in possible worlds has been so radical, though. There have also been a variety of what Lewis called ersatz possible worlds suggested by philosophers who wished to get the benefits of Lewis's possible worlds without the huge ontological cost; in this kind of theory possible worlds are generally claimed to be set-theoretic constructions of various kinds. In *linguistic ersatzism*, for example, worlds are claimed to be sets of Russellian propositions. Instead of a Lewisian possible world in which a flesh-and-blood Elizabeth II is wise, for example, we have a set of Russellian propositions, one of which is ⟨Elizabeth II, wisdom⟩.

Given that we have possible worlds of some kind at our disposal, why should the meanings of sentences be sets of them? There are two kinds of reason, which we might call conceptual and empirical. I will examine them in turn.

The main conceptual reason for construing sentence meanings as sets of possible worlds has to do with the tight connection between meaning and truth. If you know the meaning of a declarative sentence, then *ipso facto* you know what conditions would have to obtain for it to be true—to use a technical term, you know the *truth conditions* of the sentence. Conversely, if you hear a sentence and thereby grasp its truth conditions, it seems that you must have understood it; you must, in other words, have grasped its meaning. This close correspondence between sentence meaning and truth conditions has led many philosophers, led by the American Donald Davidson (1917–2003), to propose that the meaning of a sentence just is its truth conditions.

The truth conditions of a sentence, we said, are the conditions in which it is true. But what kind of thing are 'conditions' in this case? The following argument, versions of which have been given by David Lewis and the American philosopher Robert Stalnaker, gives us good reason to identify them with possible worlds. What must the meaning of a declarative sentence be able to do? (Or what must we be able to do with it?) Well, if we know the meaning of a declarative sentence, we can tell whether that sentence is true or false in any scenario that is presented to us, provided we are given enough relevant detail; and this includes imaginative counterfactual scenarios. In other words, the meaning of a sentence is something that enables us to tell whether the sentence is true in the actual world or in various merely possible worlds. What is the minimal thing that a sentence meaning would have to be in order to do that? It would have to be a set of possible worlds, the set of possible worlds in which the sentence in question was true. Thus equipped, we can scan the set, as it were, and tell whether or not any possible world that we contemplate is in there. So at a minimum, the meaning of a sentence must be the set of possible worlds in which the sentence is true; and being economical constructors of theories we will assume that that is all the meaning of a sentence is, until given reason to suppose otherwise.

There is, then, a certain amount of conceptual plausibility to the idea that sentence meanings are sets of possible worlds. But the theory, as you will not be surprised to hear, also suffers from some drawbacks. Most serious, perhaps, is its treatment of necessity. Some sentences, it is widely supposed, are *necessarily true*: they could not have failed to be true, and so, in a paraphrase widely accepted among philosophers, they are true in every possible world. *Two plus three equals five*, a defender of this theory will urge, is surely true in every possible world, since there is no possible world in which it is not the case that two plus three equals five; and the same applies to *Three plus four equals seven*. But if *Two plus three equals five* and *Three plus four equals seven* are both true in every possible world, the theory we have been looking at is forced to say that the meaning of each of them is the set of all possible worlds. The theory predicts, in other words, that these two sentences have the same meaning. But this surely flies in the face of our intuitions. Nor is this the end of it. The same kind of objection can be launched using sentences that are *necessarily false*, such as *Two plus three equals six* and *Three plus four equals eight*. These two sentences too are predicted to have the same meaning, namely the empty set, the unique set that has no members. This, again, is hardly satisfactory.

One response to this problem, advocated by the American philosophers Jon Barwise and John Perry, is to say that sentence meanings are not sets of possible worlds but sets of possible situations. The notion of a *situation* is explicated in different ways by different philosophers and linguists. The easiest way to think about situations is as spatiotemporally delimited parts of the world (or of various possible worlds). So the confines of my office between 6pm and 7pm today would be a situation. A situation could be anything from a tiny chunk of space-time to a whole possible world the size of the actual world. (Possible worlds are just large situations, indeed *maximal* situations, according to this view.) Another way of defining the notion for the purposes of semantics is to say that a situation consists of one or more individuals instantiating one or more properties or standing in one or more relations. This avoids any explicit mention of space and time and might be useful if we want to use situations to deal with sentences that mention numbers, since, after all, if numbers exist they presumably do not occupy any space. Be that as it may, a situation semanticist would say that the meaning of the sentence *Two plus three equals five* is the set of situations in which two plus three equals five; and the meaning of the sentence *Three plus four equals seven* would be the set of situations in which three plus four equals seven. Now these sets of situations will presumably include some very large situations, even whole possible worlds; some of the situations in which two plus three equals five will also be situations in which three plus four equals seven, and will thus not be useful for telling the two sentence-meanings apart. But there will also be the *minimal* situation in which two plus three equals five: that would be the situation that contains nothing but the numbers two, three, and five, and a complex relation holding between the first two and the third, a relation that we can think of as something like 'adding up to'. In general, a minimal situation in which some condition holds contains just enough entities, properties and relations to make that condition hold—nothing more. We can see, then, that the minimal situation in which two plus three equals five is distinct from the minimal situation in which three plus four equals seven. The former but not the latter would contain the numbers two and five, for one thing. So the set of situations in which two plus three equals five is distinct from the set of situations in which three plus four equals seven, since each of these sets must contain the relevant minimal situation. So by retreating from sets of possible worlds to sets of possible situations, the erstwhile possible worlds theorist may have found a way to get round the problem about necessary truths: two sentences that were true in the same set of possible worlds (namely, the set of all possible worlds) are nevertheless true in different sets of possible situations.

What can such a semanticist say to address the problem of necessary falsehoods? If we say that the meanings of *Two plus three equals six* and *Three plus four equals eight* are the sets of possible situations in which these sentences are true, it seems that the meaning of each sentence must once again be the empty set. After all, there are no possible situations in which two plus three equals six or in which three plus four equals eight. So we seem to have reached the same implausible conclusion that we reached when we were trafficking in possible worlds. What to do? If there are no possible situations in which two plus three equals six, we had better start looking into impossible situations. Let us drop the qualifier 'possible' from our talk of situations, then, and just talk of sets of situations. So the meaning of *Two plus three equals six*, on this theory, would be the set of situations in which two plus three equals six. This would of course include the minimal such situation, the one that contains just the numbers two, three, and six, and the complex relation of adding-up-to holding between the first two and the third. Thus the set of situations in which two plus three equals six is distinct from the set of situations in which three plus four equals eight, as desired.

If situations can be impossible, we had better revisit the question of what they are. It is now more obvious than ever that we can no longer say that they are portions of space-time. And we will have to tread carefully when we say that they consist of individuals having properties or standing in relations. We cannot mean by this that they must consist of individuals having properties or standing in relations that they actually do have or stand in. We must be able to pair up individuals and properties (or relations) arbitrarily, in order to deal with any bizarre sentence that we encounter. The standard way of pairing up individuals arbitrarily, of course, is with set theory. And so one standard conception of situations (the one espoused by Barwise and Perry, for example) is as set-theoretic entities: a situation might, for example, be a set or a pair of an individual plus a property that it has. If you think that this sounds suspiciously like a Russellian proposition, you are right. It does. But the Russellian theory and the situation-theoretic theory are still distinct. Take the sentence *Four is even*. The Russellian theory would say that the meaning of this sentence was the ordered pair consisting of the number four and the property of being even: $\langle 4, \text{evenness} \rangle$. The kind of situation-theoretic theory we are now contemplating would say that the meaning of this sentence is the set of situations in which four is even, with situations now being construed as set-theoretic matchings of individuals and properties. So the minimal situation in which four is even would certainly be a member of the set and would be either $\langle 4, \text{evenness} \rangle$ or $\{4, \text{evenness}\}$, depending on whether we wanted to use ordered pairs or ordinary sets. But the meaning of *Four is even* would also contain all the other situations in which four is even. For example, it would contain the minimal situation in which four is even and five is odd; the minimal situation in which is four is even and five is even (since we are now allowing impossible situations); the minimal situation in which four is even, five is odd, and the moon is made of green cheese; the whole actual universe; and so on, infinitely.

If this is now starting to sound utterly bizarre, it might help to retrace the steps that brought us to this pass. Recall the close connection between meaning and truth-conditions, the explication of truth-conditions in terms of possible worlds, and the retreat from possible worlds to set-theoretically construed situations in the face of sentences that seem to be necessarily true or false. Recall also the comforting possibility of construing all this set talk as talk about the nature of mental representations of a certain kind, using the unreasonable effectiveness of mathematics to represent the concrete world.

But it is perhaps by means of an example of it actually explaining some intricate facts about a natural language that the hold that this kind of theory exerts can most adequately be illustrated. To this, I now turn.

The permissibility of certain words and phrases in English sentences seems to depend on the presence of other words or phrases that can roughly be characterized as negative. Compare, for example, the following sentences, which I will number for ease of reference:

(1) a. Richard had not met any classicists.

    b. *Richard had met any classicists.

Example (1a) is perfectly natural but (1b) is ungrammatical. (We indicate this with the prefixed asterisk.) Since the sentences differ only by the omission of the word *not*, this word must be doing some essential work in the first sentence. What work? Let us compare the following pair of sentences:

(2) a. Richard had not met many classicists.

    b. Richard had met many classicists.

Unlike the first pair, both sentences here are perfectly fine. In particular, (2b) is perfectly fine, even though it differs from (1b) only by the addition of the letter *m*; that is, by the substitution of *many* for *any*. So we can deduce that *any* is the culprit in (1b). This word evidently needs to appear in special conditions if it is not going to render a sentence ungrammatical and these special conditions were fulfilled in (1a) by the presence of the word *not*. It seems that *not* licenses the presence of *any*. Since *any* requires the presence of negation to be grammatical, we call it a *negative polarity item* or *NPI*. The word *not* is called an *NPI-licensor*.

There are many negative polarity items in English. The following pairs of sentences contain some examples. I have put the NPI-licensor *not* in the first member of each pair (in boldface) and omitted it in the second member; in each case, observe how the second member of the pair is ungrammatical, whereas the first one is not. This is plausibly due to a negative polarity item, printed in italics, being licensed in the first members and unlicensed in the second members.

(3) a. Henry did **not** discuss the bacchanal *at all*.

b. *Henry discussed the bacchanal *at all*.

(4) a. Henry did **not** *ever* discuss the bacchanal.

b. *Henry *ever* discussed the bacchanal.

(5) a. Henry has **not** discussed the bacchanal *yet*.

b. *Henry has discussed the bacchanal *yet*.

(6) a. Henry did **not** *lift a finger* to prevent Cloke being incriminated.

b. *Henry *lifted a finger* to prevent Cloke being incriminated.

From these alternations, we can deduce that *at all, ever, yet,* and *lift a finger* are negative polarity items.

For our demonstration of the advantages of possible worlds semantics, we will need to have some idea of what expressions other than *not* are NPI-licensors. I will concentrate on two kinds of expression: determiners (words like *some* and *all*) and phrases involving temporal adverbs (*It is never the case that*). To start with, let us examine the following sentences involving determiners and negative polarity items (*any* again):

(7) a. No gods show any mercy to mortals.

b. *Some gods show any mercy to mortals.

c. *All gods show any mercy to mortals.

d. At most three gods show any mercy to mortals.

Most English-speakers find that (7b) and (7c) are severely degraded in comparison with the others. Again, this looks like a case of unlicensed negative polarity items: it seems that *no* and *at most three* at the start of a sentence license negative polarity items in the direct object, but *some* and *all* do not. Now let us compare some sentences with temporal adverbs:

(8) a. It is never the case that a god shows any mercy to mortals.

    b. *It is sometimes the case that a god shows any mercy to mortals.

    c. *It is always the case that a god shows any mercy to mortals.

Rather strikingly, the sentences with *sometimes* and *always*, just like the ones with *some* and *all*, do not seem to license negative polarity items, whereas *never* (like *no*) seems to be up to the job.

Can we give any precise characterization of the words or phrases that can act as NPI-licensors, rather than relying on the rather vague term 'negative', a term, moreover, that does not obviously apply at all to cases like *at most three gods*? The American linguist William Ladusaw proposed that NPI-licensors are all and only the phrases whose meanings are *downward entailing*. In order to appreciate what it is to be downward entailing, we will need a couple of conceptual tools. Firstly, it is necessary to start thinking of meanings in terms of extensions. As you will recall from Chapter 1, the extension of a term is the set of individuals that fall under it. So the extension of *chair* is the set of chairs; the extension of *red* is the set of red things; the extension of *walk* is the set of things that walk; and so on. (This is not the whole story about meaning, of course, as we saw in Chapter 1; but at the very least meanings can be said to determine extensions, and extensions are a legitimate semantic concept.) We also need the notion of *entailment*: roughly speaking, if one sentence entails another, there is no possible world in which the first sentence is true and the second sentence is false; if the first sentence is true, then so, automatically, is the second. For example, *Esmerelda is a vixen* entails *Esmerelda is a fox*, but not vice versa, since Esmerelda could possibly be an unfortunate male fox so-named in fit of whimsy; we assume that names are being used to refer to the same individual each time in cases like this.

Thus equipped, we can look at a case of downward entailment:

(9) a. No gods worry.

    b. No gods worry about income tax.

Example (9a) entails example (9b). There is no possible world in which (9a) is true and (9b) is false. And we can go further and say something about why this entailment holds: worrying about income tax is just a special case of worrying; since we are told in (9a) that no gods worry at all, we know a fortiori that no gods worry about income tax. In set-theoretic terms, we are told in (9a) that no god is in the set of worriers; the set of worriers about income tax is a subset of the set of worriers, i.e. is wholly contained within it; so since we know that no gods are in the set of worriers, we can be certain that no gods are in the set of worriers about income tax.

Let us pause for a very brief update in our ongoing tutorial on set theory for those who have been worrying about other things. A set B is a subset of a set A (in symbols, $B \subseteq A$) if and only if there is no object that is a member of B that is not also a member of A. So $\{1, 2, 3\}$ is a subset of $\{1, 2, 3, 4\}$; $\{1, 2, 3, 4\}$ is a subset of $\{1, 2, 3, 4\}$, and, in general, every set is a subset of itself; and the empty set, the unique set with no members, is a subset of $\{1, 2, 3, 4\}$, and, indeed, of every set. There is no object that is a member of the empty set that is not also a member of $\{1, 2, 3, 4\}$ for the very good reason that there is no object that is a member of the empty set. End of update.

Now we are in a position to appreciate the definition of downward entailment. The notion is rather general, but for our purposes, we can consider the case of phrases that combine with one other phrase to produce sentences. (For example, *no gods* combines with *worry* or *worry about income tax* to produce the sentences in (9).) Call such phrases *one-place sentence functors*. In concise and slightly technical terms, a one-place sentence functor O is downward entailing if and only if, for all phrases A and B, if the meaning of B is a subset of the meaning of A, then the sentence composed of O and A entails the sentence composed of O and B. If you are not used to reading technical definitions in linguistics, philosophy, or logic, you will be forgiven for feeling that a light mist has settled over your brain right around now. Let us go back and apply this definition to our examples. The one-place sentence functor *no god* (O) is downward entailing because whenever we have a pair of verb phrases like *worries* (A) and *worries about income tax* (B), such that the meaning of the second one (B)

is a subset of the meaning of the first (*A*), the sentence you get when you combine *no god* with the first ((9a) in our example) entails the sentence you get when you combine *no god* with the second ((9b) in our example). Feeling better now? It might help further if we consider the visual metaphor inherent in the term '*downward* entailing'. Think of looking down into Dante's Inferno, with its descending concentric circles of sinners. If you look carefully, you might be able to make out the simoniacs down in the eighth circle. If we make a generalization about the people in Hell, such as *No saint is a person in Hell*, we can look down from Hell as a whole into its eighth circle and find a subset of the people in Hell, the simoniacs, and conclude that no saint is a simoniac in Hell. Thus we see that *no saint*, like *no god*, is downward entailing.

So *no god* is downward entailing. What about the other determiner phrases we looked at? Inspection of the following examples, can help us. (I repeat the one we just looked at.)

(10) a. No gods worry. No gods worry about income tax.

     b. Some gods worry. Some gods worry about income tax.

     c. All gods worry. All gods worry about income tax.

     d. At most three gods worry. At most three gods worry about income tax.

Let us ascertain whether the first sentence in these cases entails the second. This is the case in (10a), as we just saw. It is not the case in (10b), since it is possible that some gods should worry but none worry about income tax in particular—the concerns of the gods who worry might lie elsewhere. The same holds in the case of (10c): all the gods might be worrying about things other than income tax. But in the case of (10d) we have an entailment again: if at most three gods worry at all, then for sure we know that at most three gods worry about income tax (and it may be none). So out of the current examples, *no gods* and *at most three gods* are downward entailing. And these are exactly the phrases that are NPI-licensors.

What about the phrases incorporating temporal adverbs, like *It is never the case that*? Here the advantage of thinking of sentence meanings as sets of possible worlds becomes apparent. These phrases, like the ones we just looked at, also combine with other phrases to create sentences; it is just that they combine with whole sentences (subordinate clauses) rather than with verb phrases. So they too are one-place sentence functors. So we should be able to apply the definition of downward entailingness that I just gave. Recall that a one-place sentence functor O is downward entailing if and only if, for all phrases A and B, if the meaning of B is a subset of the meaning of A, then the sentence composed of O and A entails the sentence composed of O and B. In order to see how the definition applies in this kind of case, let us examine the following examples:

(11) a. It is never the case that Zeus eats meat.

b. It is never the case that Zeus eats corned beef.

The set of possible worlds in which Zeus eats corned beef is a subset of the set of possible worlds in which Zeus eats meat. Why? Because there is no member of the set of possible worlds in which Zeus eats corned beef that is not a member of the set of possible worlds in which Zeus eats meat. So, in possible worlds terms, the meaning of *Zeus eats corned beef* is a subset of the meaning of *Zeus eats meat*. Now let us examine what the definition of downward entailingness says about this case. It says that *It is never the case that* is downward entailing if and only if, for all phrases A and B, if the meaning of B is a subset of the meaning of A, then the sentence composed of *It is never the case that* and A entails the sentence composed of *It is never the case that* and B. Now that is certainly the case with this example: the meaning of *Zeus eats corned beef* is a subset of the meaning of *Zeus eats meat*, and *It is never the case that Zeus eats meat* does indeed entail *It is never the case that Zeus eats corned beef*. Of course the definition talks about 'all phrases A and B'. So we might want to check a few more examples. For example, the set of worlds in which no mammals exist is a subset of the set of worlds in which no humans exist. (There is no member of the set of worlds in which no mammals exist that is not a member of the set of worlds in which no humans exist.) And (12a) does indeed entail (12b), just as we would predict with the hypothesis that *It is never the case that* is downward entailing.

(12) a. It is never the case that no humans exist.

b. It is never the case that no mammals exist.

So unless someone comes up with some counterexample that has not been noticed, we can assume that *It is never the case that* is indeed downward entailing.

As before, we should look at all the relevant examples:

(13) a. It is never the case Zeus eats meat. It is never the case that Zeus eats corned beef.

b. It is sometimes the case that Zeus eats meat. It is sometimes the case that Zeus eats corned beef.

c. It is always the case that Zeus eats meat. It is always the case that Zeus eats corned beef.

In the case of (13a), as we have seen, the first sentence entails the second. But in the case of the other two examples, as you can verify, this is not the case. And, lo and behold, we observed earlier that *It is never the case that* licenses negative polarity items whereas the other two phrases do not. Combining the results from (10) and (13), and comparing them with our observations about NPI-licensors in (7) and (8), we have found a perfect correlation between downward entailingness and NPI-licensing. The correlation has been extended in the technical literature to a host of examples we have not looked at.

Ladusaw's theory of NPI-licensing is pleasingly neat, then. It is significant in a number of ways. Firstly, note that when faced with sentences like those in (7) and (8) our sense that some of them are odd and some of them are just fine is instantaneous and unthinking. And yet if Ladusaw's theory is true, some part of our brain is performing set-theoretic calculations in order to reach those conclusions. If you had not heard of Ladusaw's theory before you read this, and if you are not used to thinking about set-theoretic arcana, it might have taken some mental effort on your part to understand it; but some part of your brain, a part that is inaccessible to you, evidently already knew it. This is good evidence for the *modularity of mind*, a position advocated by Noam Chomsky and Jerry Fodor according to which the mind is composed (at least in part) of many interacting specialized modules, the internal workings of which are inaccessible to each other and to consciousness.

The second way in which Ladusaw's theory is important concerns what is sometimes called the *architecture of linguistic theory*. Recall that the whole phenomenon of negative polarity is on the face of it a syntactic one: certain combinations of words (including *any*, for example) just do not form grammatical English sentences. So if the current theory is on the right lines, we have found that the syntax of English is sensitive to semantic facts: that is to say that what combinations of words form grammatical English sentences is dependent on semantic facts about them, and rather abstract set-theoretic ones at that. This has interesting implications for people speculating about the overall shape of the grammar of English, which naturally includes the interrelations between different parts of it, like syntax and semantics.

Lastly, we have also arguably found out something about sentence meanings. Ladusaw's theory is pleasingly neat and economical because it provided one definition of downward entailingness that accounted for what appeared to be two quite different types of cases: cases where a determiner plus noun combined with a verb phrase, and cases where a phrase involving a temporal adverb combined with a whole subordinated sentence. (And there are other types of cases too, which I have not tried to show you.) But this pleasing unification depended crucially upon the theory that sentence meanings were sets of possible worlds. Without that, we would not have been able to treat the relationship between *Zeus eats meat* and *Zeus eats corned beef* as formally identical to the relationship between *worry* and *worry about income tax*. So to the extent that the current theory is supported, we have evidence in favour of the possible worlds view of sentence meaning.

Tempting as it is to end there, a couple of additional notes are in order. You may be thinking that it serves no purpose showing the possible worlds theory in a good light when we observed earlier that it faced insuperable difficulties with sentences that are necessarily true or false. But recall that the theory that sentence meanings are sets of situations, to which we retreated, still has a place for possible worlds: possible worlds are just large situations of a certain kind.

And finally, it must be admitted that Ladusaw's theory of NPI-licensing is not without its problems, as with every theory in semantics. The following sentence sounds quite natural and contains the negative polarity item *any*.

(14) *(Bitterly)* Exactly four people gave me any help!

But *exactly four people* is not downward entailing, as we can tell from the following sentences:

(15) Exactly four people worry. Exactly four people worry about income tax.

The first sentence of (15) obviously does not entail the second. It is uncertain what should be done about examples like this (of which more could be adduced). One possibly relevant observation is that (14) only sounds good when it is said with certain exasperated tone, as indicated in the parenthetical stage direction. The implication seems to be that the speaker thinks that four people is not many people under the circumstances. And if we check the downward entailingness of *not many people* we find a more encouraging result:

(16) Not many people worry. Not many people worry about income tax.

The first sentence of (16) does indeed entail the second. So perhaps the door is open for a slight variant of Ladusaw's theory that would keep its essence while dealing successfully with examples like (14).

But there is no consensus in the field about exactly what should be done. As often happens in semantics, our conclusion must be a qualified one: Ladusaw's theory of NPI-licensing is impressively precise and economical, and has been extended to deal with a very wide variety of examples, but not quite all; to the extent that it is supported, the possible worlds conception of sentence meaning is also supported; but there is much still to play for.

5

Semantic properties
of sentences

In this chapter I will describe some semantic properties of sentences.
I will concentrate on entailment, presupposition, and ambiguity.

We have already met entailment in the last chapter. There I said
that if one sentence entails another, there is no possible world in
which the first sentence is true and the second sentence is false.
Equivalently, if the first sentence is true, then so, necessarily, is
the second. I gave the example of *Esmerelda is a vixen* entailing
Esmerelda is a fox, but not vice versa (since Esmerelda could be an
oddly named male fox).

One slightly unsatisfactory aspect of this treatment was that I had
to stipulate that the name *Esmerelda* was being used to refer to the
same individual each time. Obviously, if I say *Esmerelda is a vixen*,
referring to a fox of my acquaintance, this will not entail the truth
of *Esmerelda is a fox* as spoken by someone who is referring to a
different individual entirely. (That person could be mistaken and
could be talking about a tawny dog.) This phenomenon also arises
with pronouns: *He is walking fast* does not entail *He is walking* if *he*
is being used to refer to a different person each time; but it does, of
course, if *he* is being used to refer to the same person each time.

We could simply go on talking about sentences entailing other
sentences, being careful to specify the referents of any pronouns or
names as we go. And this is a widespread policy. But in order to
avoid this slight messiness, it is also common to say that entailment
is not really a relation between sentences but is rather a relation
between sentence meanings or propositions. Recall from Chapter 2

that a proposition is the meaning of a declarative sentence. It is easiest, perhaps, to think about propositions in this context as being Russellian. A simple version of the theory of Russellian propositions would say that names and pronouns, on any given occasion of use, contribute individuals to the propositions expressed by the sentences containing them. So an utterance of *Esmerelda is a vixen* would have as its meaning a Russellian proposition that paired a particular individual with the property of vixenhood: ⟨Esmerelda, vixenhood⟩. This proposition would be said to entail the proposition ⟨Esmerelda, foxhood⟩, where the very same individual is paired with the property of foxhood. Now although in writing this down I had to specify that the very same individual appeared in both propositions, this was merely an aid to the reader. The situation here is very different from the situation we find when we are talking not about Russellian propositions but about sentences: in the first position of the sentence *Esmerelda is a vixen*, all we have is a word, a word that can plausibly be used to refer to many different individuals of the same name; whereas in the first position of the Russellian proposition ⟨Esmerelda, vixenhood⟩, even though I have to write it the same way and cannot magically put a real live fox on the page before you, we do not have a word but a sharp-toothed furry animal. When we inspect Russellian propositions, then, we know who we are talking about with a certain directness that does not obtain when we merely talk about sentences, and specifications that words are to refer to the same objects are in principle unnecessary.

Entailment is used in the definition of *presupposition*. Informally, for a sentence to presuppose a certain proposition is for it to take it for granted in a certain way. (We might prefer to say that people using the sentence have to take the proposition for granted in a certain way, but I will not insist on this distinction for current purposes.) More formally, a sentence whose meaning is a proposition p presupposes a proposition q if p entails q and the negation of p also entails q. For example, *John has stopped drinking* entails that John drank. John cannot have stopped drinking unless he was drinking to start with. And *John has not stopped drinking*, the negation of the previous sentence, also entails that John drank, at least on its most natural reading.

(It is also possible to say, with a certain amount of pedantic emphasis, 'John has not *stopped* drinking because he never *started* drinking'; but this interpretation only occurs to people after a while, if at all.) So, on its most natural reading, at least, *John has stopped drinking* presupposes that John drank.

This property of presuppositions, that both the original sentence and its negation entail the presupposed proposition, makes presuppositions in a sense hard to escape from. This fact lies behind the old chestnut about the lawyer who asks a defendant, 'Have you stopped beating your wife?' The form of the question demands an answer of yes or no; but whichever one the defendant chooses, he will be tacitly admitting that he has been beating his wife. Why? Because an answer of yes is short for 'Yes, I have stopped beating my wife' and an answer of no is short for 'No, I have not stopped beating my wife'; and both answers presuppose that he has been beating his wife. This kind of example has a long history. The Megarian school of Greek philosophy in the third century BC favoured the version 'Have you stopped beating your father?' The medieval philosophers toned the example down somewhat to 'Have you stopped beating your donkey?' But then in modern times wives supplanted donkeys. (Nowadays, in a nod to gender equality, one occasionally sees the example cited as 'Have you stopped beating your spouse?') As the American linguist Laurence Horn says, the history of this example 'represents a discouraging commentary on twenty-three centuries of progress in social sensitivity.'

The sources of presupposition are many and varied. *Factive verbs* like *know, find out,* and *regret* generally introduce a presupposition to the effect that the sentence that follows them is true, as discussed already for the case of *know* in Chapter 1. A sentence like *Richard found out that Henry was concealing things from him* (or a speaker who uses it) presupposes that Henry was indeed concealing things from Richard; and similarly with *Richard regrets that Henry is concealing things from him.* If I say *It was in Vermont that our innate depravity revealed itself,* I presuppose that our innate depravity has revealed itself and assert that Vermont was the venue for this event; similarly, if I say *It was our classics professor who tipped us over the edge*, I presuppose that we have been tipped over the edge and assert that our classics professor was responsible. Sentences of this form (*It was X that did Y* or *It is X who does Y*) are called *clefts*, and they quite generally introduce presuppositions. The same can be said of the eruditely named *pseudo-clefts*: sentences of the form *What did Y was X* or *What does Y is X*, like *What ruined Henry was hubris*. But in these the presupposition resides, as it were, in the first part of the sentence, so that in the last example we presuppose that Henry was ruined and assert that the cause was hubris.

In some cases there is vigorous debate as to whether a presupposition is present. One of the most problematic cases is the apparently humble word *the*. To start with some areas of agreement, almost all modern analyses agree that existence and uniqueness are essential components of the meaning of the word. If I say, 'The King of France is bald', at any time after 1848, then what I say is not true, because there is no King of France. Similarly, if I mistakenly believe that there was one King of Sparta in 479 BC (in fact there were two), and opine, on the basis of my scanty knowledge of ancient history, 'The King of Sparta in 479 BC was worried about the Persians', then my utterance is gravely deficient. It seems that in order for any utterance of the form *The so-and-so is such-and-such* to be true and felicitous, there must be exactly one so-and-so.

I should mention a complicating factor before we go on. If I am in a room that contains exactly one table, I can gesture towards it and say, quite truly and felicitously, 'The table is covered with books.' This is so even though we know quite well that there is more than one table in the world. What is going on? It turns out to be a tricky question, one to which part of Chapter 7 is devoted. But it is as if we somehow narrow down the range of things that are to be considered when we judge whether or not there is exactly one table, and we understand the sentence rather as if I had said, 'The table in this room is covered with books.' A similar phenomenon occurs with other determiners too. If you ask me how my dinner party went and I reply, 'Everyone had a good time', you will not understand me to mean that everyone in the universe had a good time. This general phenomenon is called *quantifier domain restriction*.

These characteristics of the word *the* were used effectively in a US senate campaign in 2010, when the long-time Pennsylvania senator Arlen Specter switched from the Republican Party to the Democrats. *The Economist*'s 'Lexington' columnist tells us what happened next:

He lost a Democratic primary on May 18th to Joe Sestak, a veteran of three wars, but a relative newcomer to politics, having been elected to Congress in 2006. The ad that sank Mr Specter's campaign began, simply: 'I'm Joe Sestak, the Democrat.' Seldom has the definite article been so well-aimed.

Note, first, that quantifier domain restriction is essential to narrow down the claim to contenders in the Democratic primary: Mr Sestak was presumably not claiming to be the only Democrat in the world. And once this is achieved, the uniqueness entailment of the definite article kicks in to the detriment of Mr Specter.

Given that existence and uniqueness form part of the meaning of the word *the*, the question is how they are involved. There are two main positions here. Bertrand Russell claimed that a sentence of the form *The so-and-so is such-and-such* could be paraphrased as 'There is exactly one so-and-so, and it is such-and-such.' In other words, a speaker using a sentence of this kind would be *asserting* that there was exactly one so-and-so. For example, *The King of France is bald* means 'There is exactly one King of France and he is bald', according to Russell. Spoken at any time after 1848, then, this sentence would be false, on this analysis: it claims, among other things, that there is exactly one King of France when there is, in fact, none. Opposed to this theory are Gottlob Frege and the English philosopher Peter Strawson (1919–2006), who claimed that someone saying *The so-and-so is such-and-such* would be *presupposing* that there was exactly one so-and-so, not asserting it. If the presupposition is true, the theory goes, then the definite description *the so-and-so* refers to the unique so-and-so. The sentence then asserts that that individual is indeed such-and-such.

How can we distinguish between these two theories? It is unlikely to be much help to concentrate on sentences that are felicitous and true. Take *The Pope is Catholic*, for example. Speakers of English will, predictably, aver that this sentence is true. But this is not very useful to the theorist. We do not know whether the sentence is true because it means 'There is exactly one Pope and he is Catholic'; or, on the other hand, because it presupposes the existence of exactly one Pope and, this presupposition being satisfied, asserts that he is Catholic. Both analyses predict that we end up with a true sentence.

So it is a good idea to look at cases where things start to go wrong. Let us return to the King of France. The sentence *The King of France is bald* is predicted by Russell to be false, as we just saw. What prediction is made by Frege and Strawson? They say that the sentence presupposes that there is exactly one King of France. Since there is not, the presupposition is false. But the presupposition is not the same as the whole sentence. It is just an aspect of the meaning of the whole sentence. So we should look at sentences that uncontroversially have false presuppositions in order to see what happens with them. Consider the sentence *John has stopped drinking*, and suppose that John never drank. (We must understand the sentence to mean something like 'John has stopped drinking significant and possibly unhealthy amounts of alcohol', then.) If John never drank, is it true or false to say *John has stopped drinking*? As we saw in the discussion above, we feel some disquiet at saying either. To say either *John has indeed stopped drinking* or *John has not stopped drinking* strongly implies that John has been drinking. What we would like to say, really, is that *John has stopped drinking* is neither true nor false under the circumstances. Since he never started, the question of his stopping just does not arise. So it seems, to judge from this example at least, that sentences with false presuppositions are judged to be neither true nor false. Returning to our original train of thought, then, it seems that Frege and Strawson predict *The King of France is bald* to be neither true nor false.

You have presumably by now formed a judgement about which theory best accords with your own intuitions. But I have to tell you, with a heavy heart, that whatever your intuition is there will be plenty of people who have the opposite one. When I conduct informal surveys on this question with large roomfuls of people (when I am giving classes or talks on the word *the*), my impression, if you will pardon such unscientific methods, is that about a fifth or a quarter of the people who raise their hands think the sentence is false and the rest think that it is neither true nor false. A clear majority favour Frege and Strawson, then. But this is not a football match. We cannot say, in other words, that because Frege and Strawson have the higher score they win. We would ideally like to come up with a theory that explains all the intuitive judgements.

One possibility that should be considered is that there is a dialect difference. In other words, just as some people say *to-mah-to* and some people say *to-may-to*, some people have a Fregean definite article in their mental lexicon and some people have a Russellian one. Since the two are pronounced the same and have very similar meanings, this theory would say, the difference is not usually noticeable, and only surfaces in response to apparently senseless questions about non-existent monarchs.

Before I mention another theory, we should look at one more piece of data. If we change the example to *The King of France slashed my tires this morning*, pretty much everyone agrees that the sentence is false, even those who declined to say that *The King of France is bald* is false. Now it is Frege and Strawson who are on the defensive, since Russell's theory now appears to make a correct prediction whereas theirs would not predict any difference between the two sentences. And Russell's theory was correct for some people with respect to the first sentence. So should we say that Russell is basically correct and that some interfering factor distorts things for some people in the case of baldness?

Interestingly, the best theory on this question that I know of argues exactly the opposite. The American linguist Peter Lasersohn and the German linguist Kai von Fintel suggest that we look at things as follows. The Frege–Strawson theory is basically correct for all speakers of English. The difference between the two examples lies in the fact that being bald does not obviously affect things around you, whereas slashing someone's tires does. So when we hear *The King of France slashed my tires this morning*, two factors are relevant to its truth or falsity: first is the false presupposition, which would ordinarily make the sentence qualify for neither truth nor falsity; but second is the fact that if someone had slashed my tires this morning, then my tires would be slashed, and they are not. This second factor is enough to push the sentence over the edge, as it were, into falsity. It is as if we think, 'Even if there were a King of France, we would still know that he had not slashed my tires this morning, because my tires are perfectly intact.' No comparable factor is present in the case of *The King of France is bald*. Meanwhile, the basic judgement on *The King of France is bald*, according to this theory, is the same for all speakers at some unconscious level: the sentence is judged as a presupposition failure. That is, it is claimed that at some unconscious level there is indeed a three-way distinction between truth, falsity, and presupposition failure. But a minority of speakers, we can add, interpret the English word *false* as meaning 'not true'; for them, it thus covers both straightforward falsity (which is when an assertion is false) and presupposition failure (which is when a presupposition is false). And so they say that the sentence is false and thus appear, misleadingly, to be evincing a Russellian reaction.

The Lasersohn–von Fintel theory is complex and subject to challenges from increasingly tricky attempted counterexamples that I have not described here. It is fair to say, I think, that it has not convinced many supporters of Russell's theory to cross the floor. And indeed there is a major division within the field on this matter, which, interestingly enough, seems to track professional affiliation: philosophers, with a few exceptions, seem to favour Russell's theory of the definite article, while linguists, with few or no exceptions, favour the Frege–Strawson theory. I cannot resolve this matter here. We must be satisfied with the conclusion that telling whether or not a presupposition attaches to a sentence is not always a straightforward matter. We can also conclude that we do not know what the word *the* means, of course; but after what has gone before this will perhaps not shock you.

The last semantic property of sentences that I will examine in this chapter is ambiguity. Sentences can be ambiguous in two ways. The first is by containing one or more words that are ambiguous. So the sentence *That bank has collapsed* is in principle four ways ambiguous because of the homonymy of *bank*, and because of the polysemy of *collapse*, which could denote either physical or institutional demise. (The reading according to which a river bank undergoes institutional meltdown is hard to get, of course, because river banks are not normally the kinds of things that do this. But a Gaullist talking about Paris might refer to the organizational and moral collapse of the Left Bank in 1968.) Ambiguity of this kind is called *lexical ambiguity*, because it stems from properties of individual lexical items.

The second kind of ambiguity is called *structural ambiguity*. All the words in a structurally ambiguous sentence can have just one meaning each. So we are not dealing with lexical ambiguity. Structural ambiguity is ambiguity that arises by the meanings of words or phrases combining with each other in different ways. How can meanings combine with each other in different ways? It is best to illustrate with an example.

Consider the following sentence:

(1) Old men and women are law-abiding.

This is ambiguous between 'Old men and old women are law-abiding' and 'Old men, on the one hand, and women, on the other, are law-abiding'. The difference boils down to whether a claim is being made about young and middle-aged women. And it is fairly easy to put one's finger on the source of the ambiguity: *old* could be taken as modifying the whole phrase *men and women* or just the word *men*.

This much is not difficult to say. But there is still a question about why *old* should be able to modify either of two different things. And there is a fairly plausible answer in this case: what appears on the surface to be just one string of words (*old men and women*) actually has two different *syntactic structures*. But what are syntactic structures?

Syntax is the discipline that produces theories about what combinations of words are possible sentences. It is tempting to look at a sentence as being nothing more than a string of words. So example (1) would just consist of *old* followed by *men* followed by *and*, and so on, with no further structure. But there is a lot of evidence that indicates that, on the contrary, some words within sentences are more tightly

73

linked to each other than others. They form units, to the exclusion of other words. Let us look, for example, at the following sentence, which illustrates a phenomenon called *ellipsis*:

(2) Henry will describe the bacchanal and Francis will too.

This sentence seems in a way to be incomplete (which is not to say that it is not perfectly grammatical). It seems as if (2) is in some way short for (3):

(3) Henry will describe the bacchanal and Francis will describe the bacchanal too.

At the very least, we can note that (2) means the same as (3) and that the two are differentiated by the presence of a string *describe the bacchanal* in (3) just before *too* and the absence of that string in (2).

Not all strings of words can play the role that *describe the bacchanal* does in (2) and (3). Compare the following attempt at a sentence:

(4) *Henry will describe the bacchanal and Francis will bacchanal too.

This is not a possible sentence of English, a fact that we indicate by the prefixed asterisk. It is exactly like (2), however, except that instead of *describe the bacchanal* we have left out only *describe the*. It seems that we have found a difficulty for the theory that sentences are unstructured strings of words. If that were the case, it is hard to see why leaving out *describe the* should be any different from leaving out *describe the bacchanal*. Could omissions of two words be quite generally ungrammatical, while omissions of three are fine? Consider the following examples:

(5) *Henry will describe the bacchanal and Francis bacchanal too.

(6) Henry will describe Richard and Francis will too.

(7) Henry will describe Richard and Francis will describe Richard too.

In (5) it looks like the three-word string *will describe the* is omitted, if we compare it to (3); but this example, unlike (2), is not a well-formed

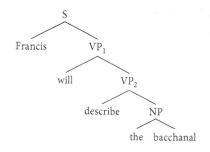

Figure 5.1 Tree diagram of *Francis will describe the bacchanal*

sentence. And if we compare (6) to (7) it looks like the two-word sequence *describe Richard* is omitted, but this is quite fine. So whatever makes (2) good and (4) bad, it has nothing to do with the length of the omitted strings of words.

There seems to be some other property that *describe the bacchanal* has that *describe the* does not. As I said above, the words *describe the bacchanal* seem to be tightly linked to each other in a certain way, in that it is possible to do something with them that cannot be done with the substring *describe the*. Contemporary syntactic theory says that the words *describe the bacchanal* form a *constituent*, whereas the words *describe the* do not. This is best appreciated by means of a diagram. Figure 5.1 shows a simplified version of the syntactic structure that would be given to the sentence *Francis will describe the bacchanal* by contemporary linguistics. This kind of figure is called a *tree-diagram*. It consists of labelled points, called *nodes*, joined together by lines, called *branches*. The nodes include the words at the bottom of the tree (you see that this tree is upside-down, with its leaves below everything else), and also the points labelled with abbreviations: S for 'sentence', VP$_1$ and VP$_2$ for 'verb phrase one' and 'verb phrase two', and NP for 'noun phrase'. A constituent, which is the crucial notion for current purposes, consists of a node plus everything that is below it, where by 'everything that is below it' I mean 'everything that you can get to by starting at the labelled node and travelling down branches'. So the whole

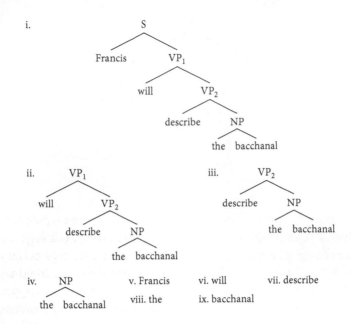

Figure 5.2 The constituents of the tree in Figure 5.1

sentence is a constituent, because the whole sentence is the node labelled S plus everything below it; and likewise the two verb phrases and the noun phrase are constituents, as are the individual words. (Individual words are nodes, and an individual word plus everything below it just amounts to the individual word, since there is nothing below the words.) Figure 5.2 lists all the constituents in 5.1. It can be seen, then, that the string *describe the bacchanal* consists of all the words in the VP₂ constituent, whereas there is no constituent whose words are just *describe the*. This, according to contemporary syntactic theory, goes at least part of the way towards explaining the difference between these two strings when it comes to ellipsis: ellipsis is performed only on constituents; we arrive at (2) by starting with (3) and omitting the lower verb phrase (VP₂) of the second sentence.

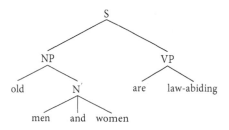

Figure 5.3 First structure of *Old men and women are law-abiding*

After this whirlwind introduction to syntactic theory, we are now ready to go back to *Old men and women are law-abiding*. The generally held theory here is that this sentence has two meanings because it has two different syntactic structures. Alternatively, we could say that we are really dealing with two different sentences that happen to contain the same words in the same order. The first structure would be that shown in Figure 5.3. The words *men and women* form a constituent labelled N′ (pronounced 'en-bar'—but the names of the labels do not matter for present purposes). Now is a good time to recall our discussion of compositionality from previous chapters: the meaning of a sentence or a phrase depends on the meanings of the words that make it up and their syntactic arrangement. The idea is that the meaning of a phrase is built up in a process that tracks the syntactic structure of the phrase. So in this case we start with *men and women* and build a meaning for that. Exactly what the meaning is does not matter, but we can think of it as being the property of being composed of both men and women. Then, following the syntactic structure, *old* comes along, as it were, and modifies this. Since both men and women are already implicated in the meaning that *old* operates on, we end up with the meaning whereby both the men and the women are old.

The second structure for this example would be that shown in Figure 5.4. Here there is no constituent that contains the words *men and women* by themselves. Instead we have a constituent formed from *old men*. The word *old* modifies only *men*, then; and so we end

77

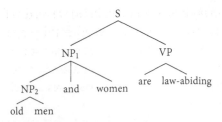

Figure 5.4 Second structure of *Old men and women are law-abiding*

up talking about old men, on the one hand, and women (of whatever age) on the other.

Structural ambiguities, then, can result from one string of words having more than one syntactic structure associated with it. They arise in many linguistic environments. Here is another example:

(8) John put the block in the box on the table.

This could be an instruction to put the block in a certain place, namely in the box on the table; or it could be an instruction to put a certain block, namely the block in the box, in a certain place, namely on the table. The ambiguity arises as follows. The verb *put* is generally followed by two phrases: the first is the direct object, indicating what is being put somewhere; and the second is a prepositional phrase or a word like *there*, indicating where the thing is question is being put. (A *prepositional phrase* is a phrase consisting of a preposition followed by a noun phrase—something like *on the table, under the bridge*, or *in an altered state of consciousness*.) In an example like *Put it there* we have a very brief version of this construction; in *Put twenty chartreuse iguanadons in the small drawing room*, the phrases are longer, but there is no obvious structural ambiguity. But when this characteristic of *put* is combined with another fact, ambiguity becomes rife. The other fact is that nouns in English can form a constituent with a following prepositional phrase and thereby be modified: I might ask how much is the *doggie in the window* or for-

78

mulate a *reply to my critics*. So when in (8) we read as far as ... *put the block in the box* ... we do not know whether the prepositional phrase *in the box* is the second phrase required by *put* or a mere modifier of *block*. The exact syntax of *put* is very difficult to ascertain; but I give simplified versions of the syntactic structures associated with these two readings of (8) in Figure 5.5.

Adding another prepositional phrase to this example complicates things even more:

(9) John put the block in the box on the table in the kitchen.

This is at least three ways ambiguous. Did John put the block in a certain place, namely in the box on the table in the kitchen? Or did he put the block that was in the box in a certain place, namely on the table in the kitchen? Or did he rather put in the kitchen a certain rather exhaustively described object, namely the block in the box on the table? The syntactic structures involved here can be seen in Figure 5.6; the triangles in these diagrams are a commonly used device to show constituents whose internal structure is not of current interest.

In fact the above meanings are not the only ones possible for (9). It is possible to construe at least some of the prepositional phrases as adverbial—as describing the action denoted by the verb, in other words. Compare *John sat on the table* and *John ran in the kitchen*, where *on the table* and *in the kitchen* tell us where the sitting and running took place. In (9), then, another possible meaning is 'John put the block in the box, and this action took place while he was on the table in the kitchen'—while he was sitting on the table, for example. The box need not have been on the table and might never have left John's hands. And finally the sentence could be paraphrased 'John put the block in the box on the table, and this action took place in the kitchen.' There are two things to note here. Firstly, the table need not be in the kitchen on this reading, just the action of putting; perhaps John is in the kitchen and is operating some robotic arms in another room by remote control. And secondly, we should recognize that there are two meanings that accord with this paraphrase, because the first part of the paraphrase, 'John put the block in the box on the

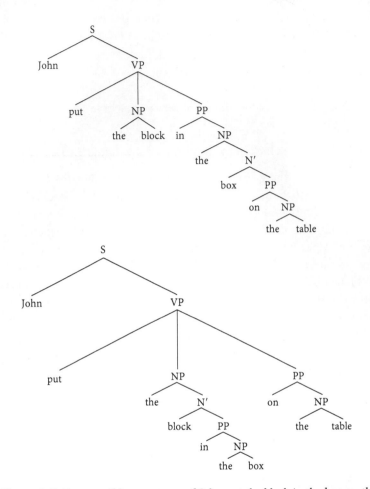

Figure 5.5 Two possible structures of *John put the block in the box on the table*

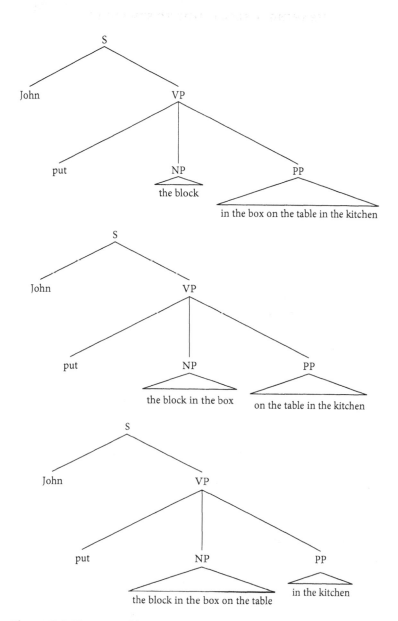

Figure 5.6 Three possible structures of *John put the block in the box on the table in the kitchen*

table', is itself ambiguous in the way that we have seen. So the sentence seems to be six ways ambiguous as a result of structural ambiguity. Add in polysemy (*table* as a graphical representation with columns and rows) and the sentence is at least twelve ways ambiguous.

If you ever find yourself on a long train journey with no reading material, you might like to try working out how many meanings can plausibly be attributed to *John put the block in the box on the table in the kitchen in the manor house.*

So far we have been examining cases where there is a broad consensus that structural ambiguities are caused by more than one syntactic structure being possible for one string of words. There has also been little or no doubt that the cases we have examined so far have been genuinely ambiguous. Both these points are less clear in the next group of structural ambiguities. They involve a group of phrases called *quantifier phrases* that can be contrasted with a different group called *singular terms*.

A singular term is one that in a referential semantics would refer to one object. Names, pronouns, demonstratives (*this* and *that*), and definite descriptions were traditionally thought to be singular terms, and many philosophers and linguists still think this of some or all of these entities. Notice that these are all things that would appear as subjects or objects of sentences. Not all subjects and objects are singular terms, though. In particular, there are the quantifier phrases. A quantifier phrase consists basically of a *quantifier* and a noun, although the noun may be accompanied by the usual complement of adjectives and prepositional phrases. Examples of quantifiers are *a, some, every, all, each, most, two, at least three, at most four*, and *no*; and examples of quantifier phrases, then, are *a man, some woman, all cats, each assiduous student of classics*, and so on. English also has a few quantifier phrases that are written as one word: *someone, everyone, anyone, no-one, somebody, everybody, anybody*, and *nobody*. What it takes to be a quantifier is best explained in terms of their semantics, which is a rather complex matter. But for now we can think, informally, that quantifiers tell us what quantity of something does something else: *Every dog barks* tells us how many dogs bark, and similarly with *No student of classics is shocked by Aristophanes.*

Crucially, these quantifier phrases do not refer to anything in the way that singular terms do. What could be the referent of *no student of classics*? A non-existent student of classics? Someone who does not study classics? Some passages in Chapter 7 of *Through the Looking Glass* instruct us on the perils of treating quantifier phrases as if they were singular terms:

'And I haven't seen the two Messengers either. They've both gone to the town. Just look along the road and tell me if you can see either of them.' 'I see nobody on the road,' said Alice. 'I only wish I had such eyes,' the King remarked in a fretful tone. 'To be able to see Nobody! And at that distance too! Why it's as much as I can do to see real people by this light!'

'Who did you pass on the road?' the King went on, holding out his hand to the Messenger for some hay. 'Nobody,' said the Messenger. 'Quite right,' said the King, 'this young lady saw him too. So of course nobody walks slower than you.' 'I do my best,' the Messenger said in a sullen tone. 'I'm sure nobody walks much faster than I do!' 'He can't do that,' said the King, 'or else he'd have been here first.'

Lewis Carroll was a mathematics tutor at Christ Church, Oxford, and the author of two treatises on symbolic logic, and as such was well placed to insert logical lessons into his fiction.

Quantifier phrases are alleged to be involved in a wide range of structural ambiguities. Let us start by examining cases involving two quantifier phrases in a sentence. Here is an example involving the quantifier phrases *exactly half the boys* and *some girl*:

(10) Exactly half the boys kissed some girl.

This could mean that exactly half the boys have the following property: they kissed some girl or other. Or it could mean that some girl has the following property: exactly half the boys kissed her. These two claims are clearly distinct. We can tell this by constructing a scenario in which the first one is true but not the second, and then another scenario in which the second one is true but not the first. Imagine that there are ten boys and ten girls; exactly five of the boys kiss a girl, and they all kiss different girls; no further kissing takes place. Then it is true to say that exactly half the boys have the property of kissing some girl or other, but false to say that some girl has the property of being kissed by exactly half the boys. So the first reading is true and the second one false. Conversely, imagine again that there are ten boys and ten girls; one rather popular girl is kissed by exactly five boys, and one of the other boys kisses another girl; no further kissing takes place. Then it is true to say that some girl has the property of being kissed by exactly half the boys, but false to say that exactly half the boys have the property of kissing some girl or other (since six boys engaged in girl-kissing overall). So the second reading is true and the first one is false.

For reasons that will emerge in a moment, it is worth being as clear as possible about the nature of the test that we just conducted involving alternative scenarios. We showed that there were situations in which the first reading of (10) was true without the second reading being true there. What would the alternative be? The alternative would be that every situation in which the first reading is true is one where the second reading is also true. In other words, the alternative is that the first reading entails the second reading. We also showed the converse, that is that there were situations in which the second reading was true without the first reading being true there. In other words, we showed that the second reading does not entail the first reading. Overall, we showed that neither of the readings entails the other. This is very useful as a guarantee that there is a genuine ambiguity here.

Why should this be a useful guarantor of genuine ambiguity? Well, consider the following piece of linguistic theorizing. A hypothetical linguist contemplates the sentence (11):

(11) John kissed some girl.

He realizes that the sentence will be true if John kissed some girl and proceeds to propose an analysis of its meaning based on this fact. Perhaps he says that the meaning of the sentence is the set of possible worlds, or situations, in which John kissed some girl; it does not matter for present purposes. Then our hypothetical colleague realizes that the sentence will be true if John kissed some Icelandic girl. He posits an ambiguity on this basis. The second meaning of the sentence can be informally summarized as 'John kissed some Icelandic girl'; and it can be represented, perhaps, by a corresponding set of worlds or situations, if that kind of treatment is being adopted. Would this be a sound piece of linguistic analysis? Certainly not. And it is fairly easy to say why. John kissing some Icelandic girl is just one way in which the world could accord with the claim that John kissed some girl. Any situation in which John kisses some Icelandic girl is, *ipso facto*, a situation in which John kisses some girl. There is no need, then, to posit both meanings. We obtain a much more satisfactory analysis if we say that the sentence has just one meaning, the proposition that John kissed some girl, and that this proposition is vague, in the linguists' sense, between various ways that it might be true, one of which involves John kissing some Icelandic girl. The analysis is more satisfactory because of concerns about compositionality: there is no evident word in the sentence meaning 'Icelandic', and we do not now have to explain how that notion enters the meaning of the whole. And it is more satisfactory because of Ockham's Razor, in that we now have just one meaning where before we had two.

Note that the putative meaning 'John kissed some Icelandic girl' entails the meaning 'John kissed some girl'. This is just a shorthand for what we have already said, that any situation in which *John kissed some Icelandic girl* is true is automatically a situation in which *John kissed some girl* is true. So the general moral we can draw is that we should be suspicious of claims of ambiguity where one of the alleged meanings entails the other one. It might turn out, in such cases, that the sentence might have just one meaning, the one that is entailed, and that the entailing meaning is not a separate meaning at all but just a representation of one way in which the world could accord with the entailed meaning.

All this is important because it turns out that a large number of the alleged ambiguities involving quantifier phrases are of this kind. Let us consider (12), for example:

(12) Every man loves some woman.

Traditionally (in introductory logic textbooks, for example), it is claimed that (12) is ambiguous in a way very similar to (10).

According to the first meaning, every man is such that he loves some woman or other. According to the other meaning, some woman is such that every man loves her. But unfortunately the second meaning entails the first. If some very popular woman is such that every man loves her, then it must be the case that every man loves some woman or other: at the very least, every man loves the woman who is loved by all men. So it is open to us to claim that in fact this example is not ambiguous, that in fact it has only the entailed meaning. If the meaning of this sentence is just 'Every man is such that he loves some woman or other', we can claim that every man loving the same woman (the alleged second meaning) is just one way that the world could be that would make the sentence true, analogous to John kissing an Icelandic girl in the case of example (11).

It is difficult to come up with a knock-down argument against this sceptical position; and yet it is a position that is not widely held. One reason, perhaps, is the structural similarity of (12) to (10): any semantic system that treated these two differently would be significantly more complicated than one that did not; and, since (10) is undoubtedly ambiguous, this lends credence to the position that (12) is too. But the basic reason for supposing that (12) is ambiguous is that people just have a very strong intuition that it is; and in the current state of our knowledge intuitions are our only source of evidence. The best way of clarifying the intuition about (12) that I know of comes from the work of the Dutch linguist Eddy Ruys. He points out a characteristic of traditional tests like the one used above to show that (10) is ambiguous; such tests, he says, assume that we can trust native speakers to say that a sentence is true in a particular scenario. We can trust them to say that (10) is true when five out of ten boys kiss the same girl and another one kisses another girl, for example. This is all very well and good. But there is no reason, Ruys says, to assume that such intuitions are reliable only when they deal with truth; we can surely also have intuitions about sentences being false in various scenarios. As well as knowing that *Grass is green and snow is white* is true, we also know that *Grass is white and snow is green* is false, after all. So now we construct a scenario in which the alleged first meaning of (12) is true and the alleged second meaning (which

86

the sceptical position explains away) is false: there are ten men and ten women; each man loves a different woman; no other loving takes place; in particular, no woman is loved by more than one man. And we ask the following questions. Can (12) be true in this scenario? And can (12) be false in this scenario? Ruys for one answers yes to both questions; and I suspect that most linguists and philosophers would do the same. So this is evidence that (12) is indeed ambiguous: one reading has been detected by its truth, and the other by its falsity.

I have gone into some detail on *Every man loves some woman* in order to show that establishing ambiguity is not always straightforward even when the alleged alternative meanings are made clear; and also in order to underline the close theoretical connection between ambiguity and entailment. But now I will disregard such qualms and describe a range of other ambiguities involving quantifier phrases with no pause for agonizing.

The examples we have just looked at involved two quantifier phrases interacting with each other. Similar effects also arise when quantifier phrases interact with negation, conditionals, and adjectives like *certain* and *likely*. To start with, what does (13) mean?

(13) Everyone isn't here yet.

If you are like me, the first meaning that springs to mind is 'It is not the case that everyone is here yet'; some people are not here yet, in other words, but some people might be. But if you think for a moment another meaning might emerge: 'Everyone has the property of not being here yet.' According to this second reading, no-one is here yet. Now if (14) is true, what has to happen in order for John to inherit a house?

(14) If a relative of his dies, John inherits a house.

Here I for one feel no difference in salience between the following two possibilities: a certain relative of his is such that, if he or she dies, John inherits a house; and if any relative of his dies, John inherits a house. If John is eagerly scanning the ranks of his senescent relatives for sources of income, he will be a lot more satisfied with the second possibility than with the first. Now what is certain in (15)?

(15) A northern team is certain to be in the final.

This could be claiming that there is a particular northern team that is certain to be in the final; or the claim could be merely that it is certain that some northern team or other will be in the final, even though no particular northern team can at this stage be said to be certain to make it. Speakers of English dialects that allow plural verb agreement after nouns like *team* (i.e. pretty much all English dialects except American ones) might be interested to note that the second reading of (15) goes away if you change *is* to *are*.

What is going on in these cases? There is no consensus in the field. One theory takes its cue from the analysis of the cases we looked at earlier, examples like *Old men and women are law-abiding*. With these, as we saw, a plausible explanation was that one string of words masked two separate syntactic structures, and that the two syntactic structures enabled the meanings of the words to combine with each other in different ways. Could the same thing be going on here? Not obviously. If we take an example like *Exactly half the boys kissed some girl* or *Everyone isn't here yet*, there is no evident way of taking the given words in the given order and assigning two usefully different syntactic structures to them. So some linguists, led by Noam Chomsky, have proposed that sentences can have two kinds of syntactic structure: one kind, called *surface structures* give us the words that we hear in the order that we hear them; but the other kind, known as *Logical Forms*, are the structures on which semantic interpretation is based. Logical Forms are derived from surface structures by means of strict rules.

Here is an illustration. Our example *Every man loves some woman* would have the surface structure shown in Figure 5.7. This gives us the words we hear in the order that we hear them. But now, according to the hypothesis being considered, we need to derive two Logical Forms for this sentence, one for each of its meanings. (We can assume for current purposes that this sentence is indeed ambiguous.) There is one rule that we need to derive these Logical Forms, a rule called

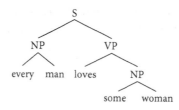

Figure 5.7 Surface structure of *Every man loves some woman*

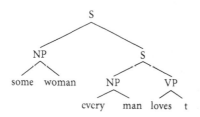

Figure 5.8 The result of applying quantifier raising to *some woman* in Figure 5.7

quantifier raising, proposed by the American linguist Robert May in 1977. Quantifier raising works as follows: take a quantifier phrase, like *some woman*; extract it from its current position in the syntactic tree and in its place put an element written 't' and called a *trace* (of which more later); form a new extended sentence by putting the moved quantifier phrase at the top-left of the tree, joined to the rest of the tree by a new pair of branches; label the revised tree 'S', since we are still dealing with a sentence, just one that we would not actually pronounce. The result of carrying out this procedure with *some woman* in Figure 5.7 is shown in Figure 5.8.

Now to derive the first Logical Form of our example we take Figure 5.8 and apply quantifier raising to it once more, this time targeting the other quantifier phrase, *every man*. The result is shown in Figure 5.9. Now how are we to interpret such an outlandish-looking structure? The advantage of this system is that it is possible

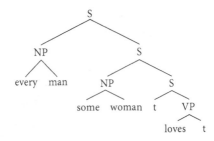

Figure 5.9 First Logical Form of *Every man loves some woman*

to provide perfectly precise and uniform interpretation rules that deliver up the meanings that are attested. Here is a version of them. In order to show that these Logical Forms yield the right interpretations, we will interpret them, as it were, into a rather formal version of English, starting at the top left. Interpret *every man* as 'every man is such that'; interpret *some woman* as 'some woman is such that'; interpret the trace left by *every man* as 'he' and the one left by *some woman* as 'she'; and interpret *loves* as 'loves'. Putting all this together, we see that this Logical Form is predicted to mean 'Every man is such that some woman is such that he loves her', which is not a bad paraphrase (if rather stilted) of the first meaning that we noted above.

It now remains to show that we can obtain the second meaning we noted using exactly the same syntactic rules and translation procedures that we have already used. (It would sound an unwelcome note of ad-hockery if we had to introduce different procedures for this reading—we want our rules to be as general as possible.) We start, as before, with the surface structure shown in Figure 5.7. As before, we apply the rule of quantifier raising to this structure twice; the only difference is that we raise the quantifier phrases in the opposite order from before. (Nothing in the formulation of quantifier raising says we have to start with any phrase in particular.) So first we apply quantifier raising to *every man* and then we apply it to *some woman*.

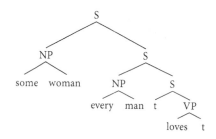

Figure 5.10 Second Logical Form of *Every man loves some woman*

The resulting Logical Form is shown in Figure 5.10. We now apply exactly the same interpretation conventions that we applied before. Starting from the top left, we end up with the following paraphrase: 'Some woman is such that every man is such that he loves her.' And this is a pretty good paraphrase of the second reading that we found for this sentence.

This kind of theory has both advantages and disadvantages. One advantage is a unified theory of structural ambiguity according to which this phenomenon is always the result of different syntactic structures. Another advantage is a fairly simple set of semantic interpretation rules. But against this kind of theory it can be urged that the syntax, with its new Logical Forms, is needlessly complicated and far removed from what we see and hear. Is it possible to account for ambiguities involving two quantifier phrases without these extra syntactic structures?

It is. But in order to get the flavour of the implementation I have in mind, it is necessary to learn one or two facts about formal logic. In order to simplify things in what will be a slightly technical exposition, I will introduce a new example that is relevantly similar to *Every man loves some woman* but less wordy:

(16) Everyone loves someone.

This is ambiguous in a way precisely analogous to the way in which *Every man loves some woman* is ambiguous. And here, in one fell swoop, is all the logic you will need:

(17) a. $\forall x Px$

   b. $\exists y Py$

   c. $\forall x \exists y\, xLy$

   d. $\exists y \forall x\, xLy$

The upside-down A, $\forall$, is read 'for all'. So (17a) is read 'For all x, P x'. It means 'For all individuals x, x has property P'. The letter x is called a *variable* and is used to range over various individuals; similarly with the letter y. The backwards E, $\exists$, is read 'there exists'. So (17b) is read 'There exists a y such that P y' and means 'There exists an individual y such that y has property P'. Suppose property P is the property of being made of paper. Then (17a) could be translated 'Everything is made of paper' and (17b) could be translated 'Something is made of paper'. Now we come to (17c) and (17d). For the purposes of these examples, we will assume that we are talking about people, so translations involving *someone* and *everyone* will be appropriate. Pieces of notation like xLy are used to talk about relations; so xLy could mean 'x loves y'. So (17c) means 'For all individuals x there is an individual y such that x loves y', or, slightly more idiomatically, 'Everyone loves someone or other'. It is a representation of the first meaning of (16), analogous to the first meaning of *Every man loves some woman* that we saw above. Meanwhile, (17d) means 'There is some individual y such that, for all individuals x, x loves y', or, more idiomatically, 'Someone is such that they are loved by everyone'. This is the second meaning of (16), analogous to the second meaning of *Every man loves some woman*. No more logic will be required.

We are now in a position to see how to obtain two readings of (16) without according it more than one syntactic structure. In fact it will not be necessary to refer to any syntactic structure at all in the theory that I am about to present—just the string of words *Everyone loves someone* will be sufficient. The theory was developed by the American linguist Chris Barker and the Taiwanese computer scientist Chung-chieh Shan.

One of Barker and Shan's crucial innovations is to represent the meanings of words as what they call *towers*, which look rather like fractions. Pieces of logical notation on the different layers of the towers come into play in different ways when whole sentences are interpreted. Here, for example, is (16) with the meaning of each word (in slightly simplified form) represented above it:

(18) $\dfrac{\forall x}{x}$ $\dfrac{}{L}$ $\dfrac{\exists y}{y}$

everyone loves someone

Barker and Shan present an algorithm for collapsing these individual meanings into one meaning for the whole that has the result, in a range of cases, that one can simply read off the meaning of the whole from initial representations like (18), starting at the top left and proceeding to the right and then down as if reading English. In this case, for example, we obtain the following meaning for the whole:

(19) $\forall x \exists y \, xLy$

And this, as you will recall from (17c) is the logical representation of the first meaning of (16).

So how do we obtain the second meaning? Barker and Shan introduce an operation called *Lift* that operates on the kinds of towers we have just seen and introduces an extra empty level anywhere except at the bottom. Taking the towers we used in (18), we use Lift to add empty layers at the top in the case of *everyone* and *loves* and in the middle in the case of *someone*. We then obtain the following representation:

(20) $\dfrac{\dfrac{}{\forall x}}{x}$ $\dfrac{\dfrac{}{}}{L}$ $\dfrac{\dfrac{\exists y}{}}{y}$

everyone loves someone

And reading from the top down in the semantic representation, as before, we obtain the following meaning for the whole:

(21) $\exists y \forall x \, xLy$

And this, of course, as we saw in (17d), is the logical representation of the second meaning of (16).

We have seen, then, that both the quantifier raising theory and Barker and Shan's theory obtain the right results, in that both predict two readings for sentences like *Every man loves some woman* and *Everyone loves someone*. Does Barker and Shan's theory have an advantage over the quantifier raising theory, in that it does not need all the extra syntactic structures of which the quantifier raising theory avails itself? In a way. The trouble is that Barker and Shan's theory, and others that have been developed along similar lines, includes complications in the semantic representations that have no counterpart in the semantics of the quantifier raising theory. They are, however, eerily reminiscent of the *syntax* of the quantifier raising theory: compare the lifting of $\exists y$ above $\forall x$, in (20), to the raising of *some woman* above *every man* in Figure 5.10. So we seem to have to make a trade-off: either we have a complicated syntax and a relatively simple semantics, or a complicated semantics and a relatively simple syntax.

It should not be thought, however, that we have come anywhere near a thorough comparison of these two strategies in this chapter. Such a project would be at the very boundaries of current research. For one thing, a wider range of examples would have to be analysed. And for another, the theories in question would have to be made more explicit in certain ways. I say something about this latter point in the next chapter.

We should not leave the topic of ambiguity, however, without noting that this phenomenon has consequences in a variety of arenas besides the theoretical. The most profound of such effects, perhaps, are to be found in law. If a statute is ambiguous, this can cause confusion regarding matters with the most urgent practical consequences.

Sir Roger David Casement (1864–1916) was said to have been 'hanged on a comma' because of the unclarity of the language in the statute by which he was convicted. He was an Irishman who held a variety of British diplomatic posts in Africa and South America; Ireland, of course, was part of the British Empire during his lifetime. Retiring from the diplomatic service in 1913, he began to show an interest in Irish nationalism, and in November 1913 became an early member of the Irish Volunteers, a paramilitary organization that was to play a role in the Easter Rising of 1916. On several occasions in 1914 and 1915, moreover, he visited Irish prisoners of war in Limburg Lahn Camp in Germany and urged them to take up arms on the German side in the First World War. Upon being captured by the British in Ireland, he was tried for treason at the High Court of Justice in London in June 1916.

The case quickly came to revolve around the wording of the Treason Act of 1351. The Act, introduced under Edward III, was written in Norman French. But in the official translation used at the time of the Casement trial, the crucial passage read as follows. Treason is committed...

... if a man do levy war against our Lord the King in his realm, or be adherent to the King's enemies in his realm, giving to them aid and comfort in the realm, or elsewhere, and thereof be properly attainted of open deed by the people of their condition: ...

The point was that Casement was not accused of any wrongdoing in the King's realm. All his potentially treasonous activity had taken place in Germany. So did the Treason Act apply to him or not?

It appears at first that the Act applies only to activities that take place in the King's realm: 'in his realm ... in his realm ... in the realm'. But then we come to the phrase 'or elsewhere'. The defence counsel, Mr Alexander Sullivan, maintained that 'or elsewhere' should be construed as modifying 'giving to them aid and comfort'. So the comma before this phrase was rather fussy punctuation, and the whole could just as well have been written 'giving to them aid and comfort in the realm or elsewhere'. Furthermore, this whole clause was to be taken as an elucidation of the previous 'be adherent to the King's enemies in his realm'. So there were only two offences here, not three: levying war against the King in his realm, and being adherent to the King's enemies in his realm. But Sir Roger had not done anything wrong within the King's realm.

One aspect of this interpretation that does not appear to have been discussed in detail during the trial is how to reconcile the 'or elsewhere' with the defence's claim that the putative traitor had to be in the King's realm at the time of the treasonous activity. Could 'giving to them aid and comfort in the realm or elsewhere' mean 'giving to them aid and comfort while they, the King's enemies, were in the realm or elsewhere'? Could the traitor remain in the King's realm, in other words, and qualify under the Act by giving aid and comfort to the King's enemies while they were elsewhere, for example by shipping weapons out to them? My own intuitions on this point are somewhat confused, and I alternate between thinking that this is a possible reading and that it is not. The alternative is that 'in the realm or elsewhere' qualifies the act of giving; and this would allow the giving to take place outside the King's realm, which would pre-sumably mean that the potential traitor could be outside the King's realm at the time, which would in turn cause difficulties for the defence's interpretation. Another possible interpretation would be that, for the 'elsewhere' clause to kick in, the traitor had to be based in the King's realm (thus satisfying the 'be adherent to the King's enemies in his realm' clause) but was allowed to take short-term extra-realm excursions for the purpose of giving aid and comfort to the enemy. This would not have been of use to the defence, however, since Ireland, where Sir Roger was resident, was at the time part of the King's realm.

Note that in the last paragraph I interpreted 'be adherent to the King's enemies in his realm' in such a way that 'in his realm' modifies the adherence. Another reading would have 'the King's enemies in his realm' as one long noun phrase with a modifying prepositional phrase: the King's enemies in his realm, as opposed to the King's enemies elsewhere. This ambiguity too was not discussed during the trial.

Thus the case for the defence. How did the prosecution construe the crucial sentence? Here is the Attorney General, Sir Frederick Smith:

How, then, ought the words to be read? They ought, in the submission of the Crown, to be read exactly as if before the word 'giving' and after the word 'realm' in the phrase 'giving to them aid and comfort in the realm,' there were brackets, that those words, in other words, were in brackets. Let it be so read: 'If a man do levy war against our Lord the King in his realm or be adherent to the King's enemies in his realm (giving to them aid and comfort in the realm) or elsewhere.'

If there are linguistic weaknesses in the case for the defence, they are at least matched, in my view, by the acrobatic verbal stretching required by the case for the prosecution. The idea that 'or elsewhere' be taken in parallel with 'in his realm', despite an intervening clause of such length, requires a truly atrocious prose style on the part of the fourteenth-century drafter. But it is not, I suppose, beyond the bounds of possibility.

The debate, then, boils down to the resolution of a structural ambiguity. Do we have 'giving to them aid and comfort in the realm or elsewhere', as claimed by the defence? Or do we have 'be adherent to the King's enemies in his realm ... or elsewhere', as claimed by the prosecution? We can see that this ambiguity is very similar to one of those we looked at earlier: in *John put the block in the box on the table in the kitchen* (example (9)), how do we construe the final prepositional phrase *in the kitchen*? As modifying *table*? As an adverbial phrase modifying *put*? In the Casement trial, too, we have difficulty deciding the semantic role of a late-arriving phrase indicating location. And as with our previous example, the ambiguity in the Treason Act is plausibly due to the existence of rival syntactic analyses. Is a syntactic constituent formed by *in the realm or elsewhere*, as the defence would have it, or by *in his realm ... or elsewhere*, as contended by the prosecution?

The presiding judges in the original trial sided with the prosecution. Casement was sentenced to death. An appeal was heard in the Court of Criminal Appeal, London, in July 1916. The most remarkable feature of this trial was that the judge, Justice Darling, announced that he had been to the Public Record Office and had examined the original statute with a magnifying glass. He announced that he had found breaks or 'transverse lines' after the words 'in his realm' (*en son Roialme*) and 'in the realm' (*en le roialme*), just where the Attorney General required brackets to be understood. He did not present a scholarly case to the effect that transverse lines in fourteenth-century legal French were the equivalent of brackets in twentieth-century English; but this did not bode well for the accused. Roger David Casement was hanged on 3 August 1916 at Pentonville Prison.

One can only wonder that people can be heard using derogatory phrases like 'just semantics' and 'mere semantics'. They evidently do not know that semantic interpretation can, quite literally, be a matter of life and death.

6

Meaning and grammar

How do we understand a sentence that we have never encountered before? We cannot have the meaning of every sentence of English memorized in advance. For one thing, it seems that there is no upper bound on the number of English sentences. Imagine that the gods have sentenced some reprobate, perhaps someone who played loud music late at night in a residential area, to a Sisyphean punishment. Instead of endlessly pushing a boulder up a hill, this sinner must stand by an endless conveyor belt reciting the things she sees pass before her, in the following fashion: 'I have seen a comb, and a brush, and a bowl full of mush, and some mince, and some quince, and a runcible spoon, . . .', and so on, forever. (If you are worried about running out of things to put on the conveyor belt, have it go round in a circle.) It is evident that this utterance will never come to an end. But we could break it after any of the noun phrases (except the first one, *I*) and obtain an English sentence: *I have seen a comb*, *I have seen a comb and a brush*, and so on. Since the punishment of the player of loud music goes on forever, there is no limit to the number of English sentences we can obtain this way. So there is, in principle, an infinite number of English sentences. So they cannot all fit in our heads, which are, fortunately, only finitely large.

As we have already seen in Chapters 2 and 4, the answer to this problem is compositionality: the meaning of a sentence is calculated on the basis of the meanings of the words in it and their syntactic arrangement. A finite number of words is sufficient to form an infinite number of sentences, as we can see from the variant of the above scenario in which the conveyor belt goes round in a circle, meaning that the same things will recur and that the words describing them can be reused. So all we need to do to understand novel sentences is have a finite list of word meanings memorized and be able to combine the meanings of these words to work out the meanings of phrases and sentences. The previous chapter, in the discussion of the ambiguity of sentences like *Every man saw some woman*, showed some simplified versions of this process: a system of putting together informal paraphrases in stilted English, in the case of the Logical Form theory, and a system of reading off translations into formal logic in the case of Barker and Shan's theory.

It is important to emphasize that the discussion in the previous chapter was simplified in some important ways. For one thing, no-one really thinks that the meanings of sentences are paraphrases in stilted English. And no-one thinks that the meanings of sentences are strings of logical symbols, impressive though that increase in technical sophistication may have seemed at the time. We would like to see a way of arriving in a compositional fashion at things that are actually reckoned to be meanings of sentences by significant numbers of contemporary philosophers and linguists. In this chapter, then, I will provide exactly that for two such things: Russellian propositions and sets of possible worlds. Each of these, though, does dual duty: a Russellian proposition could be taken literally, as it were, as an abstract object of a certain kind, or it could be taken as a mathematical model of an internal mental representation; and similarly for sets of possible worlds. I choose the latter over the more theoretically adequate sets of situations merely because they are better established; sets of situations would work in exactly the same way.

First, though, before delving into the particulars of either one of these two theories, I will give an outline of the whole process in more general terms. The basic insight, which goes back to Gottlob Frege, is that semantic composition can be modelled as *functional application*. In order to understand this term, we need a bit of background on *functions*.

There are two ways of thinking about functions. At the most intuitive level, a function is an all-purpose device for taking something and giving something back in a rule-governed way. One of the rules in question says that a function must give back exactly one object for

Figure 6.1 The structure of *Mary swims*

any given input. For example, the well known mathematical operation of squaring is a function. If we give 1 to the squaring function, we get back 1; if we give 2, we get back 4; and so on. We say that the object taken by a function is its *argument* and the object returned is the *value* of the function at that argument; and in an ink-saving piece of notation, we pick a letter, say 'f', to represent the squaring function and write '$f(3) = 9$' for 'the value of the squaring function at argument three is nine'. We also say that this function *maps* 3 to 9, and, in general, each number to its square. We can also think of functions as sets of ordered pairs. The squaring function on the natural numbers would be the infinitely large set of ordered pairs that included $\langle 1, 1 \rangle$, $\langle 2, 4 \rangle$, $\langle 3, 9 \rangle$, and so on, with the arguments appearing as first members of the pairs and the values as second members. But for present purposes, the first, more dynamic, conception of functions is more helpful.

Functional application, then, is applying a function to an argument to obtain a value. In our example above, with the squaring function written 'f', we can apply f to 1 and get 1, we can apply f to 2 and get 4, and so on. Frege's basic idea is that the meanings of some words are, or can be modelled as, functions; they apply to the meanings of other words and the value that they return is the meaning of some larger phrase.

As an example, let us take the sentence *Mary swims*. This sentence has the simplified structure in Figure 6.1. We know the meaning of the whole sentence is going to be the proposition that Mary swims. We are forgetting for the moment the various ways that propositions can be analysed. And let us assume, for the sake of simplicity, that the meaning of the word *Mary* is just Mary, a particular woman. Somehow we need to combine the meaning of *swims* and the meaning of *Mary* to arrive at the proposition that Mary swims; and we are going to be guided by Frege's theory and say that this combination takes place by the meanings of some words being functions. Since the meaning of *Mary* is not a function, but just a woman, this means that the meaning of *swims* must be a function. What must it be able to do? In this instance it takes Mary as its argument and gives us back the proposition that Mary swims. On another occasion, however, we might be dealing not with *Mary swims* but with *John swims*; and then we want to obtain the proposition that John swims. So the meaning of *swims* must be able to take any individual as argument. To be precise, it must be a function that takes an individual as its argument and gives back the proposition that that individual swims. In slightly more formal terms, the meaning of *swims* must be a function that takes an individual x and gives back the proposition that x swims.

Strictly speaking, I should say that the meaning of *swims* is the *smallest* function that takes an individual x and gives back the proposition that x swims. By 'smallest' here, I mean simply that the function does this and nothing else. There could be a function that mapped any individual x to the proposition that x swims and also mapped the Mona Lisa to the square root of -1. But it would be rather extravagant to suppose that the meaning of *swims* had anything to do with the Mona Lisa or the square root of -1. So we want the smallest function that does what we need. In the rest of this chapter, I will write things like 'the function that maps so-and-so to such-and-such' and mean by that 'the smallest function that maps so-and-so to such-and-such'.

I will shortly show how this idea would be implemented with respect to Russellian propositions and sets of possible worlds. But first it will be convenient to introduce some notation to write down functions in a perspicuous and brief manner. The standard notation for writing down functions in mathematics, computer science, and linguistics is called the *lambda notation*; it was invented by the American mathematician Alonzo Church (1903–1995). Instead of writing 'the squaring function' we will write '$\lambda x.x^2$'. The first symbol here, 'λ', is the Greek letter lambda. An expression that begins '$\lambda x.$' is a function that takes an argument x and maps it to whatever comes after the dot. So $\lambda x.x^2$ takes an argument x and maps it to x^2. We sometimes write functions in square brackets with their arguments following in parentheses, as follows:

(1) $[\lambda x.x^2](4)$
   $= 4^2$
   $= 16$

It is sometimes helpful to think of applying a lambda term to an argument as a purely formal operation; an operation, in other words, that manipulates pieces of notation. The '$\lambda x.$' on the first line of (1) reaches out, as it were, and places the argument, '4', in place of any occurrence of 'x' that follows; the '$\lambda x.$', having done its task, then drops away and we are left, in this instance, with '4^2'.

Here are some more examples. The functions in these cases take a number and add it to itself; take a number and use it as an exponent (the superscript added to numbers when squaring them or cubing them, or whatever); and, in the last case, take a number and map it to another function:

(2) $[\lambda x.x + x](5)$
   $= 5 + 5$
   $= 10$

(3) $[\lambda x.2^x](3)$
   $= 2^3$
   $= 8$

(4) $[\lambda x.\lambda y.x^y](3)(2)$
   $= [\lambda y.3^y](2)$
   $= 3^2$
   $= 9$

The last example is slightly more complex than the others. But it works in exactly the same way. The initial '$\lambda x.$' reaches out to the first argument it finds ('3' in this case) and puts it in the place of any occurrences of 'x' that follow; it then drops out as usual. There is only one occurrence of 'x' after the '$\lambda x.$', so we are left with '$\lambda y.3^y$'. Now this is itself a function, as we can tell by the '$\lambda y.$' at the beginning. This works in exactly the same way as 'λx', with the exception, naturally, that it takes an argument and puts it in the place of any occurrences of 'y' that follow (not 'x'), before dropping out. Doing this, we are left with '3^2'. We will shortly see that some English words, transitive verbs, behave very like the first function in (4) in that they too take an argument and map it to a function, which then takes another argument; the two arguments are the meanings of the subject and object of the verb, in the case of transitive verbs.

Returning to *Mary swims*, I will now show how functions enable us to arrive at the interpretation of this sentence in a compositional manner, starting with the theory of Russellian propositions. In this theory, we want the meaning of the whole sentence to be the Russellian proposition that pairs Mary with the property of swimming, as shown in (5):

(5) ⟨Mary, swimming⟩

The meaning of *Mary*, as I said, I will assume to be just a particular person, Mary. So the meaning of *swims* must be a function that takes an individual x and maps it to the Russellian proposition that pairs x and the property of swimming:

(6) $\lambda x.\langle x, \text{swimming}\rangle$

This function takes Mary as its argument and we obtain the desired outcome:

(7) $[\lambda x.\langle x, \text{swimming}\rangle](\text{Mary})$
 $= \langle \text{Mary}, \text{swimming}\rangle$

As usual, we can think of this calculation either as I introduced it just before example (6), or as a manipulation of pieces of notation: the initial 'λx.' reaches out and takes the argument, 'Mary', and puts it in the place of any occurrences of 'x' that follow; it then drops out.

Let us go on to see how this compositional version of the Russellian theory would deal with an example involving a transitive verb. Example (8) would have the structure in Figure 6.2.

Figure 6.2 Structure of *Mary sees Fido*

(8) Mary sees Fido.

Syntacticians reckon that the verb forms a constituent with the object, to the exclusion of the subject; this is partly in order to maintain the overall subject-predicate structure that must be present in *Mary swims* and other examples with intransitive verbs.

Let us treat names, once more, as simply standing for individuals. So *Mary* refers to a particular woman, Mary, and *Fido* refers to a particular dog, Fido. As before, then, the verb must stand for a function in order to compose the disparate meanings of the individual words into a whole. We also know what meaning we want to end up with, although I have not yet introduced Russellian propositions of this kind. The Russellian proposition that would be the meaning of (8) is the following:

(9) ⟨⟨Mary, Fido⟩, seeing⟩

This proposition is the ordered pair whose members are ⟨Mary, Fido⟩, on the one hand, and the relation of seeing, on the other. The first member of the pair is itself a pair. We have to adopt a convention about the order in which the members of this first pair will be put. In practice, the order adopted tends to be the order in which the members of the pair are represented in the English sentence in question—so Mary comes first because the word *Mary* precedes the word *Fido*—but we could if we liked come up with a more semantic principle with which to order the two. We could say, for example, that in the case of verbs of perception, like *see*, the perceiver comes first and is followed by the perceived. The proposition will be true if and only if the relation that is its second member holds between the members of its first member, with those considered in the manner stipulated. In this case, then, it will be true if and only if Mary sees Fido; Fido seeing Mary will not be sufficient.

What we need then, for the meaning of *sees*, is a function that will apply to Mary or Fido and eventually, perhaps via an intermediate stage, give us (9). But before we write down this function, we have to make a choice. In the case of *Mary swims* there was no option but to have the meaning of *swims* apply to the meaning of *Mary*. After all, there was nothing else around that it could possibly have targeted. But in the present case we could in principle have the meaning of *sees* apply to either Fido or Mary. Which one should we choose?

The universal convention, which seems to work out very well in empirical terms, is to have the meaning of *sees* apply to the meaning of *Fido*. These two words form a constituent, the verb phrase. They are also said, in syntactic jargon, to be *sisters*. Take the VP node in Figure 6.2. It is possible to travel down from there to either of *sees* or *Fido* without meeting any other nodes on the way. The nodes *sees* and *Fido* are thus said to be *immediately dominated* by the VP node; and any nodes that are immediately dominated by the same node are sisters. The family tree metaphor should be obvious. The hypothesis for composing meanings can now be stated in more general terms: semantic compositionality is functional application between sisters. In other words, the meaning of one sister will take the meaning of the other one as an argument; and the value returned will be the meaning of the immediately dominating node.

In this case, then, we need to have the meaning of *sees* be a function that will take as its argument the meaning of *Fido* and give back something that will be an appropriate meaning for the VP as a whole. This VP meaning will look across, as it were, to its sister, which is *Mary*, and take the meaning of this word and give back something that will be an appropriate meaning for the node that immediately dominates *Mary* and VP, i.e. for the sentence as a whole. With no further ado, here is something that will do this for the case of Russellian propositions:

(10) $\lambda x.\lambda y.\langle\langle y, x\rangle, \text{seeing}\rangle$

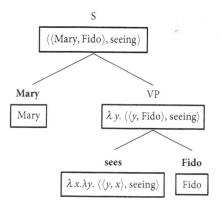

Figure 6.3 An annotated version of *Mary sees Fido* showing the meanings in Russellian terms

This function takes the meaning of *Fido*, i.e. Fido, as its argument:

(11) $[\lambda x.\lambda y.\langle\langle y, x\rangle, \text{seeing}\rangle](\text{Fido})$
     $= \lambda y.\langle\langle y, \text{Fido}\rangle, \text{seeing}\rangle$

The resulting function, $\lambda y.\langle\langle y, \text{Fido}\rangle, \text{seeing}\rangle$, according to our procedure, is the meaning of the VP. It then takes as its argument the meaning of its sister:

(12) $[\lambda y.\langle\langle y, \text{Fido}\rangle, \text{seeing}\rangle](\text{Mary})$
     $= \langle\langle \text{Mary}, \text{Fido}\rangle, \text{seeing}\rangle$

The value thus returned is the meaning of the whole sentence. It was what we were aiming for, as a quick glance back at example (9) will confirm. Figure 6.3 contains an annotated syntactic tree for the current example with all the meanings of the various nodes enclosed in boxes; the original words are now in bold.

Before we examine the possible worlds approach to propositions, it will be convenient to introduce one more piece of notation. As well as listing the members of sets, as in (13), we can also define them by a method sometimes known as *abstraction*, as in (14):

(13) $\{2, 3, 4, 5, 6, 7, 8, 9\}$

(14) $\{x|x > 1 \text{ and } x < 10\}$

Assuming that we are talking about the natural numbers, these two definitions pick out the same set. The second one is read, 'The set of entities x such that x is greater than one and x is less than ten.' Instead of listing the members of the set, we have specified a condition that must be fulfilled in order to be in the set.

Armed with this notation, we see that the possible worlds approach to propositions deals with compositionality in a very similar fashion to that adopted by the Russellian theory. It would say that *Mary swims* has as its meaning the proposition in (15):

(15) $\{w|\text{Mary swims in } w\}$

This picks out the set of worlds w such that Mary swims in w; or, in other words, the set of possible worlds in which Mary swims. How do we arrive at this meaning compositionally? We claim that *swims* has the meaning in (16):

(16) $\lambda x.\{w|x \text{ swims in } w\}$

Applying this function to Mary, the meaning of *Mary*, we obtain the meaning of the sentence:

(17) $[\lambda x.\{w|x \text{ swims in } w\}](\text{Mary})$
     $= \{w|\text{Mary swims in } w\}$

Proceeding to *Mary sees Fido*, we posit the following meaning for *sees*:

(18) $\lambda x.\lambda y.\{w|y \text{ sees } x \text{ in } w\}$

As previously, this function applies to Fido, the meaning of *Fido*:

(19) $[\lambda x.\lambda y.\{w|y \text{ sees } x \text{ in } w\}](\text{Fido})$
     $= \lambda y.\{w|y \text{ sees Fido in } w\}$

The resulting function, $\lambda y.\{w|y \text{ sees Fido in } w\}$, is the meaning of the VP. It applies to Mary, the meaning of *Mary*:

(20) $[\lambda y.\{w|y \text{ sees Fido in } w\}](\text{Mary})$
     $= \{w|\text{Mary sees Fido in } w\}$

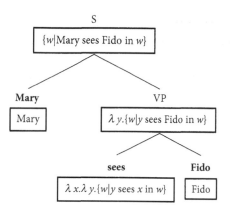

Figure 6.4 An annotated version of *Mary sees Fido* showing the meanings in possible worlds terms

As before, the desired result is obtained. Figure 6.4 contains an annotated version of the structure of *Mary sees Fido*, showing the meanings of the various nodes in possible worlds terms.

There is, of course, much more to English than names and simple transitive and intransitive verbs. But I will not attempt to show how to give compositional accounts of sentences involving other kinds of words. The examples given so far will hopefully be enough to give the flavour of the enterprise.

In conclusion, I should perhaps emphasize once more that exactly what we take ourselves to be doing in giving an account like this will depend on what we think meanings are. If we favour the referential theory of meaning, we might think that we are speaking literally when we say that verb meanings, for example, are functions: we might think that the meanings of some words are mathematical entities of exactly this kind, and presumably, therefore, abstract objects. We might think that we have improved upon the version of the referential theory given in Chapter 2, whereby the meanings of verbs and other predicates were properties or relations. In order to explain compositionality, we have now amended this account to say that the meanings of verbs are functions that manipulate properties and relations.

If we favour the internalist theory of meaning, we cannot take ourselves to be speaking literally when we say that verb meanings are functions. For functions, as I said, are abstract objects, if they exist. We will rather maintain that we are using 'the unreasonable effectiveness of mathematics in the natural sciences' to give a mathematical model of the behaviour of some very interesting parts of our heads. We will therefore inherit the problem of spelling out what exactly it means for mathematics to do this and how it might be expected to be able to do it; but we will note that this problem is shared by all the sciences. I will not attempt to resolve it here.

7
Meaning and context

The previous chapters have proceeded as if words and sentences had just one kind of meaning. This simplification will now be abandoned.

A very basic observation will start us off. Some words, as we have seen, are plausibly used to refer to people or things. Such words include names, pronouns, and demonstratives (*this* and *that*). Other examples include *here, there, now, then, today,* and *tomorrow,* which are plausibly used to refer to places and times. Now at least some of these words are used to refer to different objects on different occasions of use. The pronoun *she,* for example, can be used to refer to any female person (as well as ships and, occasionally, countries and cars). The pronoun *I* is generally used by speakers to refer to themselves, *you* is used to refer to someone whom one is addressing, and so on. Since lots of different people speak and lots of different people are addressed, these pronouns are used to refer to different people on different occasions. The same holds of *this, that, here, there, now, then, today,* and *tomorrow*: if I use the word *today* today, it will pick out one particular day (15 November 2010, as it happens); if I use it tomorrow, it will pick out a different one; and similarly with the other examples.

The only possible exception to the generalization that referring terms can pick out different things on different occasions is constituted by names. Some theorists think that there is one name *John,* for example, and that it can be used to pick out any one of a large number of people who are so named. If this is the case, *John* is like *he,* in that it can be used to refer to different people on different occasions. But other theorists think that there are lots of homophonous words pronounced 'John', one for each person called John, so that each name is used of only one person. Since there is disagreement on this point, we will concentrate on other examples.

In addition to occasions of use, we will also talk about words being used to refer to different objects in different *contexts of utterance*, where a context of utterance is the set of circumstances in which a sentence is spoken or written; it will typically include the identity of the speaker, the identity of the addressee (if any), the place and time of the utterance, and perhaps other things. Words that can be used to refer to different objects in different contexts of utterance are called *indexicals*.

Indexicals can be used to make a rather fundamental point about the nature of meaning. Suppose that on 15 November 2010 John sincerely says, 'I am tired today.' Suppose further that on 16 November 2010 Mary also says, 'I am tired today.' According to the ideas about meaning that we have been examining so far, these two utterances would have different meanings. In possible worlds terms, John's utterance would have as its meaning the set of possible worlds in which John is tired on 15 November 2010; whereas Mary's utterance would have as its meaning the set of possible worlds in which Mary is tired on 16 November 2010. These are clearly two different sets of possible worlds. If we prefer Russellian propositions, the meaning of John's utterance will contain John as a constituent (and not Mary) while the meaning of Mary's utterance will contain Mary (and not John). So we are clearly dealing with two different propositions, however we construe them.

Nevertheless, it cannot be denied that in some sense John and Mary said the same thing. They both said, of themselves, that they were tired on the day of speaking. Imagine, to change the scenario slightly, that you walk into a classroom and find the words *I am tired today* written on the blackboard, without any clue as to who wrote them. If all there was to meaning was the kind of meaning that was illustrated in the last paragraph, then you would not know the meaning of that sentence. The reason is that you would not know who the word *I* was supposed to be referring to: you would not know who to insert as the relevant constituent of a Russellian proposition, or whose tiredness levels to pay attention to when drawing up an appropriate set of possible worlds. Analogous things can be said about *today*. But this conclusion is plainly nonsense. In a very important way, you do know the meaning of the sentence *I am tired today*, even if you do not know who wrote it or spoke it.

The two kinds of meaning just illustrated were influentially discussed by the American philosopher David Kaplan, who called them content and character. The *content* of an utterance of a declarative sentence is the kind of thing that we have been concentrating on before this chapter. Formally, we have been representing it in terms of sets of worlds or situations, or by means of Russellian propositions. Intuitively, we can think of it as the claim that is made by the speaker in saying the sentence in question. John was claiming that he, John, was tired, and so John himself has to feature somehow in the content of this utterance of the sentence. You do not know the content of *I am tired today* if you just come across those words written on a blackboard with no clue as to who wrote them.

On the other hand, you do know the *character* of that sentence. You know, in this case, that someone was claiming, of themselves, that they were tired on the day of writing. (Of course, the sentence might also have been written as an example sentence during a semantics class. Let us ignore this possibility. Imagine that it was written by a student experiencing existential angst.) The character of a sentence can be thought of as the meaning contributed by the words themselves, irrespective of the context of utterance. More specifically, in Kaplan's theory, given a particular utterance of a sentence, the character of the sentence is something like a rule or procedure for examining the context of utterance and arriving, on that basis, at the content of the utterance of the sentence. In the case of John uttering *I am tired today* on 15 November 2010, the character has to take note of two aspects of the context of utterance: the utterer of the sentence (because it contains the word *I*); and the day of the utterance (because the sentence contains the word *today*). In other words, the character of a sentence has to make provision for assigning referents to all the indexicals that the sentence contains. On this basis, we can arrive at the content of the utterance in question: that John was tired on 15 November 2010. The same procedure with a different context of utterance will yield up the different content associated with the sentence when Mary says it the day after John did.

If we feel so inclined, we can of course model this talk of procedures by means of functions. Functions are, after all, procedures that might be said to arrive at certain outcomes on the basis of certain inputs. In Kaplan's theory, then, the character of a sentence is a function that takes the context of utterance as its argument and returns, as its value, the content of the sentence in that context. For example, the character of *I am tired today* would be the function that takes a context of utterance and returns the proposition that the person speaking or writing in that context is tired on the day of that context. All such propositions will involve particular people or days: for example, the proposition that John was tired on 15 November 2010 and the proposition that Mary was tired on 16 November 2010. Indexicals, according to Kaplan, contribute particular individuals to propositions; he summarizes this attribute by calling indexicals *directly referential*.

Kaplan reckons that individual words have characters too, and that these too are functions from contexts of utterance to content. For example, the character of the word *I* is a function that takes a context of utterance and gives back the speaker in that context. So when John is speaking, it gives back John. The character of a verb like *swims* will be a function that takes a context of utterance and gives back the content of the word *swims*, where the content of this word is one of the meanings given for it in the previous chapter.

Assuming that issues of compositionality can be resolved, can we conclude that Kaplan's theory gives something like the whole picture regarding indexicals? Unfortunately not, as he himself admits. The problem is that Kaplan's theory, as just mentioned, deals only with what he called directly referential uses of indexicals—only, that is, with occasions on which speakers refer to some particular object by means of an indexical. Once again, it is useful here to think of Russellian propositions: the kinds of cases we have been dealing with are those in which an indexical does nothing other than contribute a particular person or thing to a slot in one of these ordered pairs.

The problem is that not all uses of indexicals can be analysed in this way. Take third-person pronouns, for example. They have referential uses, as in (1). But what is going on in (2)?

(1) *(With a gesture at Benedict XVI)* He is the Pope.

(2) Every boy believes he deserves ice cream.

Example (2) could involve a referential use of the word *he*, of course. Perhaps the speaker is referring to Benedict XVI and claiming that every boy believes that Benedict XVI deserves ice cream. But this is not the only possible interpretation. The sentence could also be used to assert that every boy believes himself to deserve ice cream—a very different proposition. And it is clear that this latter reading cannot involve a referential use of *he*. What could *he* possibly be referring to on this reading? The set of all boys? But then the speaker would be claiming that every boy believes that the set of all boys deserves ice cream, which is something very different. Example (2) does not necessarily involve every boy believing something about all boys— only something about himself.

The pronoun in (2) has what is called a *bound reading* or a *bound variable reading*. It seems to depend somehow on the preceding quantifier phrase *every boy*, which is said to *bind* it. If you had an intuitive understanding of the use of the variables x and y in formal logic in Chapter 5, you will see that *he* here seems to behave very like one of these, as the following semi-formal paraphrase makes clear:

(3) Every boy x is such that x believes that $\underline{x}$ deserves ice cream.

The underlined occurrence of the variable 'x' seems to be a pretty good translation of the pronoun *he*. But can we produce any explicit description of what is going on here? Here is one way. As I said, there seems to be a crucial relation between *every boy* and *he*. Here is a modified version of (2) with these expressions removed and their positions marked:

(4) ___ believes ___ deserves ice cream

Now suppose that there are three boys: Tom, Dick, and Harry. We form new sentences by inserting the names of the boys, one by one, in the slots left by the quantifier phrase and the pronoun it binds, always inserting the same name each time in any one sentence:

(5) a. Tom believes Tom deserves ice cream.

    b. Dick believes Dick deserves ice cream.

    c. Harry believes Harry deserves ice cream.

Since we are dealing with *every boy*, our original sentence (2) can be thought of as claiming that every one of (5a)–(5c) is true. Now consider (6):

(6) Some boy believes he deserves ice cream.

This sentence can be thought of as claiming that some sentence among (5a)–(5c) is true. And this general procedure is a good way of thinking about the semantics of a pronoun when it is bound by a quantifier phrase: it provides a slot, as it were, in which all of the relevant objects are considered, one at a time, in order that some claim might be made about them. The relevant objects are the ones denoted by the noun in the quantifier phrase—boys, in this case. And the nature of the claim depends on the quantifier itself.

Another example of a non-referential occurrence of a pronoun is found in the following:

(7) Every man who owns a donkey beats it.

Here, again, in the most natural reading, *it* cannot be referential. A speaker of this sentence would not be referring to some particular donkey, Flossy, for example, and saying that every man who owns a donkey beats Flossy. There is no consensus, however, on exactly what the pronoun here does mean. One school maintains that *it* is bound, very much as in the previous example. And indeed, one can come up with a quasi-logical paraphrase for the sentence in which the pronoun does seem to be translated by a bound variable:

(8) For all x and for all y such that x is a man and y is a donkey and x owns y, x beats y.

One problem with this, however, is that it involves translating *a don-key* as 'for all y such that ... y is a donkey': it involves treating *a donkey* as if it were a universal quantifier like *every* or *all*, in other words. There are arguably costs involved in doing this: *A donkey walked in* does not mean the same as *Every donkey walked in*, after all. The other main school of thought on this problem claims that the meaning of (7) is something more like that of (9a) or (9b):

(9) a. Every man who owns a donkey beats the donkey he owns.

    b. Every man who owns a donkey beats the donkey.

The pronoun *it*, here, is claimed to have the meaning of a definite description, then. This too faces problems, perhaps most notably the fact that we now have two completely different meanings for non-referential pronouns: bound uses and definite descriptions. This is naturally very unattractive from the point of view of theoretical economy.

This phenomenon goes by the attractive name *donkey anaphora*, on the basis of (7), which is an old example. (Compare the lawyer's question about beating your wife: the older an example is, the more likely it is to involve beating something.) Anaphora is the semantic dependency between pronouns and other phrases illustrated in (2) and (7): the pronouns in these cases seem to be dependent on preceding quantifier phrases in some way for their semantic functioning. The type of dependency in (2) is sometimes called *bound anaphora* or *bound variable anaphora*. Note that there are syntactic differences between the configuration in (7) and the configuration in (2): in (2), the quantifier phrase that the pronoun was semantically linked to was the subject of the whole sentence, whereas in (7) the pronoun seems to be linked to the phrase *a donkey*, which is buried inside a relative clause attached to the subject noun. Researchers still differ on the question of how significant these syntactic differences are and, in general, on whether donkey anaphora can be reduced to bound variable anaphora.

There is, however, another kind of example where there seems to be little alternative but to have pronouns interpreted as definite descriptions. Consider (10):

(10) *(With a gesture at Benedict XVI)* He is usually an Italian.

If we heard someone say this, with the gesture indicated, we would not interpret them as claiming that Benedict XVI is usually an Italian. We would interpret them as claiming that the Pope is usually an Italian. Example (10) is synonymous with (11). It is not synonymous with (12):

(11) The Pope is usually an Italian.

(12) Benedict XVI is usually an Italian.

If we think that names are generally referential, the fact that (12) does not have the kind of reading that (10) has is an argument against supposing that *he* could somehow be referential in (10). The meaning seems rather to be that of a genuine definite description, as in (11). It seems that, under certain circumstances at least, pronouns can stand for any definite description that is made sufficiently salient by the context of utterance. Gestures at visually prominent clues, as in (10), certainly help things along. Cases like (10) are called *descriptive indexicals*.

In some sentences, the multiplicity of possible interpretations for pronouns make for an impressive degree of ambiguity. For example, how many readings does (13) have?

(13) Every journalist who ever interviewed the mayor of Arkham found that ten years earlier he had been a communist.

To start with, *he* could be referential. It could be referring to the current mayor of Arkham, or to some person being pointed to by the speaker. It could also be bound: the reading would be that every journalist who ever did that kind of interview found out that ten years earlier he himself had been a communist. This would perhaps involve the journalists suffering from amnesia and having to do research, or be reminded, in order to find out their former political convictions. Thirdly, the pronoun could be interpreted in a way rather reminiscent of donkey anaphora, so that it ranges over various mayors of Arkham. Suppose that only three mayors of Arkham have been interviewed: Angell was interviewed in 1920, Blackwood was interviewed in 1950, and Curwen was interviewed in 1990. This reading claims that the journalists found that Angell was a communist in 1910, Blackwood was a communist in 1940, and Curwen was a communist in 1980. (Note that these gentlemen do not need to have been mayor at the time of their communism.) And fourthly, there is a reading that is like the last, except that the journalists, on the occasion of each interview, found out that the person who had been mayor ten years previously had been a communist: in 1910, Armitage had been mayor and had been a communist; in 1940, Bishop had been mayor and had been a communist; and in 1980, Corey had been mayor and had been a communist. The mayors who were interviewed do not need ever to have been communists on this reading. This last reading, and perhaps the third, presumably involve the pronoun being interpreted as a definite description, 'the mayor of Arkham'.

And as if we did not already have enough meanings for pronouns, consider the following extract from J.K. Rowling's *Harry Potter and the Deathly Hallows*:

(14) *(Harry attempts to cast a spell)* Nothing happened, but he had not expected it to.

This evidently means, '…he had not expected anything to happen.' The pronoun *it*, then, seems to be able to mean 'anything'. (It is perhaps helped by the presence of the word *nothing*, which is equivalent to 'not anything'—but that is another story.) The word *anything* is a quantifier phrase. It turns out that there are other examples, too, of pronouns being able take on the meanings of quantifier phrases, although the phenomenon is quite rare. In fact I spotted the Harry Potter example because I had been alerted to such a possibility, having already spontaneously uttered a pronoun with a meaning of this kind in the following exchange with someone near and dear to me:

(15) SP: Every towel has a purpose.
       PE: No, it doesn't!

My meaning was, 'No, every towel doesn't have a purpose.' (More explicitly: 'It is not the case that every towel has a purpose.') So the pronoun *it* evidently meant 'every towel'. It appears, then, that in limited circumstances pronouns can take on contextually salient quantifier phrase meanings. This phenomenon has not yet received extensive investigation.

It is not only the third-person pronouns *he*, *she*, and *it* that display readings other than directly referential ones. All indexicals have been argued to display such readings, and, although there is more uncertainty in some cases than in others, the number of examples that are not in any serious dispute is high. Here, for example, is a donkey sentence involving the demonstrative *that*:

(16) Every man who owns a donkey beats that donkey.

Again, the indexical in question (*that donkey*) seems to mean something like 'the donkey he owns'. Here is a descriptive indexical reading of *tomorrow*:

(17) Tomorrow is always the biggest party night of the year.

This example is drawn from an article in the University of Arizona newspaper; the article appeared one year on the Friday before classes started. The example evidently means, 'The Saturday before classes start is always the biggest party night of the year.' Note that *tomorrow* cannot possibly just be referring to one particular day, say Saturday 4 September 2010: that day is not 'always' the biggest party night of the year, because that day will only ever occur in one year.

And here, to round us off, is an example of *I* not used in accordance with the direct reference theory. Recall that *I*, according to Kaplan's classic theory, just refers to the person who utters it. Various counterexamples to this claim could be given. My favourite is from the heart-rending, funny, and verbally inventive television show *Buffy the Vampire Slayer* (1997–2003). In the Third Season episode 'Doppelgängland', written and directed by series creator Joss Whedon,

Willow, one of the main characters, accidentally summons the counterpart of herself that exists in an alternate reality (or in an alternative possible world, as we would say). Among other things, it seems that Willow has been turned into a vampire in the possible world in question. There are a few other little differences too, as Willow remarks:

(18) That's me as a vampire? I'm so evil...and skanky. And I think I'm kinda gay.

Fans of the show remember this line as significant foreshadowing, in that the Willow who was native to the possible world of the show realized that she was 'kinda gay' in Season Four and became evil, not to put too fine a point on it, in Season Six. But for our present purposes, it is the use of the pronoun that is important. When Willow says 'I'm so evil', and so on, she does not mean that she, the speaker, is evil. She means that the person she is looking at across the room is evil. In that respect, it seems that Kaplan's theory of *I* needs emendation. But since the person she was looking at across the room is, in a manner of speaking, herself, we might hope that the emendation required in this case will be relatively small.

Overall, however, it is impossible to sustain the position that indexicals are only referential. Third-person pronouns and demonstratives, at least, all have bound variable, donkey-anaphoric, and descriptive indexical uses in addition to referential uses. Other indexicals, as we have briefly seen, also have uses that are at variance with the direct reference theory. A lot of current research is focused on coming up with a unified semantics for indexicals that will make all these uses fall out as special cases; but as yet there is no consensus in the field.

The action of overt indexicals like *I*, *she*, and *tomorrow* is not the only way in which the same sequence of words can have different contents in different contexts of utterance. Imagine that we are in Arkham, Massachusetts, on 1 August 2010 at 2pm. I look around me and say (19):

(19) It's raining.

You would take me to have expressed the proposition that it is raining in Arkham, Massachusetts, at 2pm on 1 August 2010. When we write it out like this it looks significantly larger than the small sentence *It's raining*. The time and date can be taken to be contributed to the proposition by the present tense of *is*, which is plausibly an indexical, working somewhat like *now*; its semantic value is the time of utterance and it contributes this to the proposition expressed. But what about the location? I was definitely claiming that it was raining in Arkham, and not that it was raining in Boston, Amherst, or anywhere else. So the location must figure, somehow, in the content of the sentence for that utterance. But how does it get in there? There are no words or parts of words in *It's raining* that obviously have anything to do with contributing the place of utterance.

Example (19) is not the only one to involve a comparable problem. In fact this phenomenon is extremely widespread. Consider the following utterances:

(20) Everyone was sick.

(21) I haven't eaten.

Imagine I held a dinner party last night and you ask me how it went. I reply with (20). Obviously you will not take me to be asserting that everyone in the world was sick. You will take me to be asserting that everyone who attended my dinner party was sick. But there is no word or phrase in (20) that can plausibly be taken to denote the property of attending my dinner party. How, then, does this property end up in the proposition expressed? Similarly, if I say (21) at 8pm you will not take me to be saying that I have never eaten in my life. You will take me to be saying that I have not had dinner that day. But I pronounce no word or phrase that means 'dinner'; and so it is mysterious how the sentence ends up meaning what it does.

These sentences are obviously similar to the cases of overt indexicals, in that, as I said, they could mean different things in different contexts of utterance. Even if we keep the time constant, (19) will express different propositions depending on where it is said. (And things are not that simple: if we are in Arkham and discussing the weather in Boston, an utterance of (19) might mean that it is raining in Boston.) Example (20) will attribute sickness to different groups of people depending on what occasion is under discussion. And (21), even if we hold the speaker constant, will claim that different meals are untasted depending on when it is spoken.

But this observation delivers up only a limited amount of insight. We are still left wondering how exactly we arrive at the meanings of these sentences. One initially promising strategy that has found advocates over the years is to imagine that a proposition is extracted from a sentence in two stages: we arrive at a content based on the words in the sentence; and then we understand that content as making a claim only about a spatially and temporally delimited part of the world—about a situation, in other words. Recall the discussion of situations in Chapter 4; the new kind of situations we are dealing with are called *topic situations*, because they are supposed to be what the sentence is in some sense about. For example, the content that we derive from the words *It's raining* might be the set of situations in which it is raining, following the proposal in Chapter 4:

(22) $\{s | \text{it is raining in } s\}$

But then in a separate and obligatory step, this content is paired up with a topic situation, which could consist of the town of Arkham at the time of utterance. And the whole proposition that is asserted is that the topic situation is a member of the set of situations that we get from the words of the sentence; in this case, that the situation consisting of Arkham at the time of utterance is a member of the set of situations in which it is raining; in other words, that it is raining in Arkham. With *Everyone was sick*, the content derived from the words would be the set of situations such that everyone in them is sick; and then the topic situation consisting of my dinner party is claimed to be one of those. And so on.

This suggestion is elegant and, in a wide range of cases, effective. But unfortunately it cannot work. Consider the following sentence:

(23) Everyone is asleep and is being monitored by a research assistant.

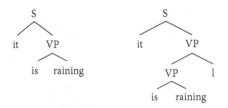

Figure 7.1 Two possible structures for *It's raining*

This might be spoken to indicate what stage an experiment on sleep has reached. The plain meaning, in the context, would be that all the experimental subjects were asleep and were being monitored by a research assistant. But can we achieve this meaning by finding a suitable content for the sentence and a suitable topic situation? The sentence's content, on the theory in question, would have to be the set of situations in which everyone is asleep and is being monitored by a research assistant. Can we find a topic situation in which that is so? Surely not. For the research assistant, in the middle of the monitoring task, is presumably not asleep. There is no situation in which everyone is asleep and the research assistant is not asleep, because 'everyone' naturally includes the research assistant.

So the content that we are looking for, which we can call *implicit content*, cannot just come in via a global restriction on the applicability of the content that we derive from the audible words of the sentence. It will have to be more closely interwoven, as it were, with the content derived from the audible words.

Some theorists respond at this point by reverting to the similarity that I mentioned between examples (19)–(21) and examples involving overt indexicals. They claim that (19)–(21), and similar examples, are interpreted by means of covert indexicals: indexicals that are present in the syntactic structure of the sentences in question but just not pronounced. For example, the claim is that (19) does not have the first structure in Figure 7.1, which is what we might have expected, but rather the second. The l in the latter tree diagram is an adverb that works exactly like *here* in that it contributes the location of the utterance to the proposition expressed; but it is unlike *here* in that it is

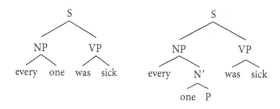

Figure 7.2 Two possible structures for *Everyone was sick*

unpronounced. In our example, 1 would end up meaning something like 'in Arkham, Massachusetts'.

Similarly, example (20), on this theory, would have not the first structure in Figure 7.2 but the second. In this structure, the constituent P is a covert indexical that is capable of taking on various properties as its semantic value. In our example, it would mean something like 'who attended Elbourne's dinner party'. We might compare the overt indexical *one* on some of its uses: with a nod at a dog behaving oddly, I might point to another and say (24):

(24) That one does just the same.

Here, of course, the meaning is 'That dog does just the same'; so the indexical *one* can sometimes have as its value properties that are salient in the context of utterance. The unpronounced constituent P in Figure 7.2 would be rather similar. And in (21) some theorists would posit an unpronounced noun phrase in direct object position just after *eaten*. Acceptance of this theory requires, of course, that we posit lexical items in the syntax that are not pronounced, a prospect that many syntacticians baulk at; but many others, including those influenced by Chomsky's latest theories, do not mind positing such things, as we saw in Chapter 5 in connection with traces.

We can now see how to deal with example (23). The first part of the sentence has the structure in Figure 7.3; the covert indexical P here has a value something like 'who is a subject in Dr Whateley's experiment on sleep'. Since the implicit content is supplied locally, as it were, there is now no need to find some situation or property that applies equally to the subjects and the research assistant.

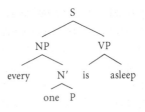

Figure 7.3 A possible structure for *Everyone is asleep*

It is possible to use the devices just described to make an interesting and far-reaching claim about the propositions expressed by utterances of sentences. But before spelling out this claim, it is worth spending a bit more time on the notion of the *proposition expressed*. In the case of (19), given the stipulated context of utterance, the proposition expressed is that it is raining in Arkham, Massachusetts, at 2pm on 1 August 2010. In the case of (20), the proposition expressed is that everyone who attended my dinner party was sick. And so on. The proposition expressed by a sentence can, then, be thought of as the claim made by the speaker in uttering that sentence. The problem posed by cases of implicit content is that the audible words do not seem to be able to yield up enough content to get us to the proposition expressed. So now we come to the claim about the proposition expressed that involves covert indexicals: it is that the proposition expressed is always the result of assigning referents or other semantic values to the words in a syntactic tree and then combining those semantic values by means of compositional rules. What pops out at the end of the compositional semantics, in other words, is the proposition expressed. The existence of cases like (19)–(21) seemed to threaten this position. But the above strategy of plugging apparent gaps by means of covert indexicals allows us to maintain it. Or so it is claimed by some theorists. This position is currently most closely associated with the American philosopher Jason Stanley.

This position was tacitly adopted in Chapter 6, where we looked at some of the mechanisms of compositional semantics. Indeed you might be wondering what the alternative is. The alternative was proposed by the French cognitive scientist Dan Sperber and the English linguist Deirdre Wilson. The most basic part of their position is the denial of the previous position. So they maintain that the proposition expressed cannot always be derived from the meanings of items in the syntax, as combined by the compositional semantic rules. But they go further. They regard the output of the compositional semantics as an object in the conceptual system, perhaps a complex concept or a string of concepts; in this they follow Chomsky, as explained in Chapter 2. Implicit content is added only at this stage. For example, (23) is subject to the compositional semantics and yields up an object in the conceptual system that we can represent as in (25), using capital letters to stand for concepts again, as is conventional:

(25) EVERYONE IS ASLEEP AND IS BEING MONITORED BY A RESEARCH ASSISTANT

This representation is not to be taken seriously, of course, as an attempt at showing how concepts really work; the essential point is that there is no mention, as it were, of being a subject in the experiment at this first stage. This contrasts with Stanley's position, according to which the implicit content makes its presence known via the syntax and would, therefore, appear in the output of the compositional semantics, since the compositional semantics operates on syntactic trees. In Sperber and Wilson's model, the representation in (25) is considered as a possible candidate for the proposition that the speaker wished to express; and if there is any reason to amend it, this can be done, again operating purely within the conceptual system. In this case, for example, the string EVERYONE IS ASLEEP cries out for emendation, since it is not the case that everyone, with no qualification (everyone in the world?), is asleep, and the speaker evidently knows this, as the mention of the research assistant makes clear. (Presumably the speaker also believes that the addressee is not asleep.) So the representation in (25) is changed to the one in (26):

(26) EVERYONE WHO IS A SUBJECT IN PROFESSOR WHATELEY'S
SLEEP EXPERIMENT IS ASLEEP AND IS BEING MONITORED BY A
RESEARCH ASSISTANT

This process is called *pragmatic enrichment* by Sperber and Wilson, whose theory as a whole is called *Relevance Theory*. *Pragmatics* is the sub-discipline of linguistics that investigates the relation between the proposition expressed and the context of utterance.

The last ten years have seen a vigorous debate between advocates of the two approaches to implicit content just outlined, but it is fair to say, I think, that no-one has yet come up with a knock-down argument in favour of either side. And note that this debate concerns only the level at which the implicit content manifests itself: is its presence reflected in the syntax or only in the conceptual system? We have not yet touched on the most mysterious question in this area, which is how we manage to work out what the implicit content is when we hear an utterance that involves it. We are seldom conscious of having to do this. The process of filling in implicit content, whether as the value of covert indexicals or the product of pragmatic enrichment, is unconscious and extremely swift. And yet the factors that might have to be taken into account are legion, and involve subtle psychological facts about what the speaker might be expected to know and wish to tell us. They include banal details about what the speaker is working on at the time, as with the example of the sleep experiment, and outré facts about the psychopathology of the speaker: compare the different interpretations that would arise from an eminent psychiatrist saying that he is having an old friend for dinner, depending on whether or not the speaker is Hannibal Lecter. We are far, to say the least, from having an explicit and detailed theory of all this.

It would not be surprising, however, were it to emerge that there is often a disparity between the implicit content that the speaker has in mind and the implicit content that the hearer supplies for the same utterance. As we saw in Chapter 2, speakers differ on the exact meanings that they give even for common, audible words; I see no prospect of their always arriving at the same solution for something that they have to fill in by complex inferential processes. As with the case of words, though, this might not always matter. If the speaker has in mind the proposition that every subject in the experiment she and the hearer are working on is asleep and the hearer arrives at the proposition that every subject in Professor Whateley's sleep experiment is asleep, this will not really matter for practical purposes, provided that Professor Whateley's experiment is the one that the speaker and hearer are working on.

But in some cases, unclarity about implicit content can have serious practical consequences. Once again, it is convenient to turn to law for an example. In *Smith* v. *United States* (1993), the United States Supreme Court upheld a thirty-year prison sentence for a small-time drug-dealer on the basis of a disputed use of the verb *use*. The petitioner, John Angus Smith, had attempted to trade a MAC-10 automatic firearm, with silencer, for two ounces of cocaine. Unfortunately for him, the person he was attempting to trade with was an undercover police officer. Still more unfortunately for the petitioner, the relevant statute, 18 U.S.C. § 924(c)(1), prescribes a five-year prison sentence for cases where a defendant 'during and in relation to' any crime of violence or drug trafficking 'uses or carries a firearm'. The sentence is to be increased to thirty years when, as in this case, the weapon is a machine gun or is fitted with a silencer.

The case naturally came to centre on the meaning of the phrase *use a firearm*. The defence maintained that this meant 'use a firearm as a weapon'. And if that interpretation had prevailed, the lower court's thirty-year sentence would have been struck down, since Smith did not discharge the gun, threaten anyone with it, or otherwise use it offensively. But the Supreme Court, by a majority of 6–3, disagreed. Here is Justice O'Connor writing for the majority:

When a word is not defined by statute, we normally construe it in accord with its ordinary or natural meaning...Surely petitioner's treatment of his MAC-10 can be described as 'use' within the everyday meaning of that term. Petitioner 'used' his MAC-10 in an attempt to obtain drugs by offering to trade it for cocaine.

[...]

In petitioner's view, § 924(c)(1) should require proof not only that the defendant used the firearm but also that he used it as a weapon. But the words 'as a weapon' appear nowhere in the statute. Rather, § 924(c)(1)'s language sweeps broadly, punishing any 'us[e]' of a firearm, so long as the use is 'during and in relation to' a drug trafficking offense...Had Congress intended the narrow construction petitioner urges, it could have so indicated. It did not, and we decline to introduce that additional requirement on our own.

This interpretation did not convince the redoubtable Justice Scalia, however. Here is part of his dissent:

To use an instrumentality ordinarily means to use it for its intended purpose. When someone asks 'Do you use a cane?' he is not inquiring whether you have your grandfather's silver handled walking stick on display in the hall; he wants to know whether you *walk* with a cane. Similarly, to speak of 'using a firearm' is to speak of using it for its distinctive purpose, i.e., as a weapon. To be sure, 'one can use a firearm in a number of ways,'...including as an article of exchange, just as one can 'use' a cane as a hall decoration—but that is not the ordinary meaning of 'using' the one or the other. The Court does not appear to grasp the distinction between how a word *can be* used and how it *ordinarily is* used. It would, indeed, be 'both reasonable and normal to say that petitioner "used" his MAC-10 in his drug trafficking offense by trading it for cocaine.'...It would also be reasonable and normal to say that he 'used' it to scratch his head. When one wishes to describe the action of employing the instrument of a firearm for such unusual purposes, 'use' is assuredly a verb one could select. But that says nothing about whether the *ordinary* meaning of the phrase 'uses a firearm' embraces such extraordinary employments. It is unquestionably not reasonable and normal, I think, to say simply 'do not use firearms' when one means to prohibit selling or scratching with them.

On the interpretation of the Court, the thirty-year sentence would presumably be applicable if a drug-dealer scratched his head with a gun fitted with a silencer as a signal to a colleague that a potential buyer of drugs had arrived on the scene.

The whole dispute, it can readily be seen, centres on whether the phrase *use a firearm* should be understood, in the context of the statute, as being accompanied by some implicit content, namely 'as a weapon'. I personally suspect that Justice Scalia was onto something when he accused the Court of not appreciating the difference between how a word or phrase can be used and how it ordinarily is used; but I would rephrase it, in the light of the preceding theoretical discussion, as a question of whether the Court recognized that a phrase can be used with some particular implicit content, even though it is not always used with that implicit content. Interesting avenues in the theory of statutory interpretation are opened up here, ones which a small number of philosophers are starting to explore.

Suppose that you are interpreting an uttered sentence. In a series of extremely intricate processes that are largely subconscious, you access the sentence's words in your mental lexicon and find their meanings; you work out the intended sense of any ambiguous words it might contain; you work out the references of the indexicals in the sentence; you work out the sentence's syntactic structure and resolve any structural ambiguities there may be; and you combine the contents of the words in the compositional semantics. (This is assuming that you are in a position to run the compositional semantics on contents; of course you might have to deal with character, which would be even more complex.) If implicit content is not mediated by means of covert indexicals (and thus covered by the second step mentioned above), you add in some of this too. Finally, you have worked out the content of the sentence, as uttered on that occasion. It all sounds exhausting (although on most occasions we do it effortlessly, of course), and you would be forgiven if you thought that you were now done with the interpretation of that utterance. But if you thought that, you would be wrong.

Suppose that you are with some friends, discussing how to spend an evening. One of the group—call her Mary—says (21), repeated here as (27):

(27) I haven't eaten.

You look up all the words in your mental lexicon, identify the reference of *I*, do the compositional semantics, and fill in the implicit content. You thus arrive at the proposition that Mary has not eaten dinner on the evening in question. But you would not have grasped what Mary was trying to communicate unless you also realized that she was hinting that she would like to go to a restaurant.

It is overwhelmingly likely, in the circumstances, that you would pick up on Mary's hint. How do you do this? In other words, why not take her merely to be giving a progress report on her calorie intake? The answer, once again, lies with the context of utterance. Since the group was in the midst of a discussion of what to do, it would have been bizarre and antisocial of Mary to interject an utterance that had nothing to do with that topic and was not, furthermore, of any urgent independent interest. (You would understand if she had gone off-topic by yelling 'Fire!', provided, of course, that there was a fire.) Unless you have some reason not to do so, you take her to be contributing to the discussion in progress. That requires looking for some way in which the utterance is relevant to that discussion. And such a way is not hard to find.

Philosophers and linguists say that Mary *implicated* that the group should go to a restaurant and that that proposition was an *implicature* of her utterance. These terms were coined by the English philosopher Herbert Paul Grice (1913–1988), who gave the following influential account of the process of implicature. Conversation, said Grice, is a rational and purposive activity. Even the most apparently casual exchange has a certain purpose or direction, even if it is only to avoid an awkward silence. The same goes, of course, for more structured verbal exchanges such as debates, tutorials, and interviews. Given this, Grice formulated a principle that he took to hold of verbal exchanges: 'Make your conversational contribution such as is required, at the stage at which it occurs, by the accepted purpose or direction of the talk exchange in which you are engaged.' He labelled this the *Cooperative Principle*.

The Cooperative Principle breaks down into four more specific maxims:

A. The Maxim of Quantity

   i. Make your contribution as informative as is required.

   ii. Do not make your contribution more informative than is required.

B. The Maxim of Quality: Try to make your contribution one that is true

   i. Do not say what you believe to be false.

   ii. Do not say that for which you lack adequate evidence.

C. The Maxim of Relation

   Be relevant.

D. The Maxim of Manner: Be perspicuous

   i. Avoid obscurity.

   ii. Avoid ambiguity.

   iii. Be brief (avoid unnecessary prolixity).

   iv. Be orderly.

On this basis, says Grice, we can now explain how we compute implicatures. The idea is that people will interpret us in such a way as to preserve the assumption that we are abiding by the maxims, if at all possible, even when we do not appear to be. In fact our appearing to violate the maxims is frequently a clue that an implicature is intended.

Mary's utterance in (27), for example, appears at first to violate the Maxim of Relation. But people will search for a way of avoiding this conclusion, and, as I explained above, we find it easy to hit upon the explanation that Mary is actually proposing that food play a prominent role in the evening's entertainment.

Here is another example involving the Maxim of Relation, one of Grice's own.

(28)   —Smith doesn't seem to have a girlfriend these days.
     —He has been paying a lot of visits to New York lately.

In order to interpret the second utterance as being relevant to the first, the first speaker must suppose that the second is citing evidence that is meant to suggest that Smith has a girlfriend in New York. And this interpretation is readily available.

Moving on to the Maxim of Quantity, imagine that you are on a university committee charged with selecting a new lecturer in philosophy and you read the following in a letter of recommendation from Mr Smith's PhD supervisor:

(29) Dear Sir or Madam, Mr Smith's command of English is excellent, and his attendance at seminars has been regular. Yours sincerely, Eva Lou Ator

I suspect that your enthusiasm for hiring Smith would decline sharply, even though nothing bad has been said about him. The writer apparently flouts the Maxim of Quantity, in that not enough information is given—nothing about how good Smith's PhD thesis is, for example, or, in general, how good he is at philosophy. But the reader, according to Grice, will reason as follows. The supervisor is being cooperative. If she were not, why would she be writing at all? She must have knowledge of how good Smith is at philosophy, because she is his supervisor. So she must be reluctant to write her opinion down. There is no reason not to write down a favourable opinion, so her opinion must be unfavourable. His supervisor, then, has implicated that Smith is no good at philosophy. And in violating one of the Gricean maxims, she has actually communicated something that she would rather not put on paper.

As an example of an implicature based on an apparent breach of the Maxim of Quality, Grice produces a nice little theory of irony. Suppose that Smith and Jones were on friendly terms, but then Jones betrays Smith in an act of vile treachery. Smith might very well say, of Jones:

(30) He's a fine friend!

Assuming that the hearers know the history of the pair, this remark will readily be perceived as ironic. How? Well, says Grice, Smith, in saying (30), is purporting to say something obviously false. His hearers know that he cannot really mean that Jones is a fine friend. So, for his utterance to have any point at all, he must be trying to convey some other proposition. And this other proposition must presumably be related to the one that is the content of the sentence he utters, since there are no other clues available. The most obvious choice is that Smith is attempting to convey the negation of the content of the sentence he utters.

The term *convey*, incidentally, is frequently used in the literature on implicature. In fact there is a pair of technical terms, *what is said* and *what is conveyed*: what is said by an utterance of a sentence, in the technical sense, is the content of the sentence on a particular occasion of use, as described above; and what is conveyed by an utterance of a sentence is what is communicated by that utterance. This may include the content (although it need not, as in the case of irony); but it will certainly include any implicated propositions.

Finally let us look at an example of an implicature based on the Maxim of Manner. Suppose that the reviewer of a concert writes (31a):

(31) a. Miss X produced a series of sounds that corresponded closely with the score of 'Home Sweet Home'.

  b. Miss X sang 'Home Sweet Home'.

The reviewer writing (31a) when he could have written (31b) is a prima facie breach of the Maxim of Manner, in particular of the sub-maxim that enjoins avoidance of unnecessary prolixity. Why would he have done such a thing? 'Presumably,' says Grice, 'to indicate some striking difference between Miss X's performance and those to which the word *singing* is usually applied. The most obvious supposition is that Miss X's performance suffered from some hideous defect.'

A distinctive and occasionally useful characteristic of implicatures is that they can be *cancelled* without contradiction. To cancel an implicature is to deny that it holds. In the case of (28), for example, the second speaker could possibly continue, 'I don't mean to suggest that he has a girlfriend in New York.' So there is a sense in which one commits oneself less irrevocably to the propositions that one implicates than to the propositions that are the content of one's utterances. This naturally makes implicatures a fit medium for all kinds of shady dealings. They are also useful in their very distinctness from content:

if one can bamboozle one's interlocutor into responding only to the content of one's utterance, a potentially damaging implicature might slide by unchallenged.

A good example of the latter strategy was to be seen on the BBC television programme *Newsnight* on 20 June 2006, when the presenter Jeremy Paxman interviewed the American political commentator Ann Coulter (of whom he transparently disapproved) about her new book:

(32) Paxman: Your publishers gave us Chapter 1, Ann Coulter. I've read it. Does it get any better?

      Coulter: Apparently a lot of people think so.

By asking whether the book improves after Chapter 1, Paxman implicated that that chapter was of low quality. (The implicature can most plausibly be seen as being based on the Maxim of Relation: why bother to ask if the book gets any better if the first chapter was just fine?) And Coulter, despite being very media-savvy and having trained as a lawyer, did not challenge the implicature, although it was clear from her facial expression that she realized that Paxman was pulling a fast one. This example is rather reminiscent of the lawyer's question about whether the defendant has stopped beating his wife: either a yes or a no in response is tantamount to an admission of guilt, and yet the question demands an answer of yes or no. It would have been more satisfactory, from Coulter's point of view, if she had answered with something like the following:

(33) Actually, a lot of people have told me that Chapter 1 is really rather good. But, to answer your question, I think that Chapter so-and-so, in which I do such-and-such, is even better than Chapter 1.

It is one thing, however, to come up with such analyses after the fact, from the comfort of one's armchair. Producing such answers within the space of a split second, in front of television cameras, is rather harder.

For an example of a conveniently cancellable implicature, let us turn to a political speech by Hillary Clinton. The venue was Portsmouth, New Hampshire, on 6 January 2008. The former First Lady was speaking in a debate organized as part of the Democratic primaries in the run-up to that year's presidential election. She spoke of her role in the Northern Ireland peace process:

(34) And I was very privileged to work on behalf of the peace process in Northern Ireland. I actually went to Northern Ireland more than my husband did. Because I was working to help change attitudes among people. Because, you know, leaders alone rarely can make peace. They have to bring people along who will believe that peace is in their interest. And I remember a meeting that I pulled together in Belfast in the town hall there, bringing together for the first time Catholics and Protestants from both traditions, having them sit in a room where they have never been before with each other. Because they don't go to school together, they don't live together and it was only in large measure because I really asked them to come that they were there, and I wasn't sure it was going to be very successful.

And finally a Catholic woman on one side of the table said, you know, every time my husband leaves for work in the morning, I worry that he won't come home at night. And then a Protestant woman on the other side said every time my son leaves to go out at night, I worry that he won't come home again, and suddenly instead of seeing each other as caricatures and stereotypes, they saw each other as human beings, and the slow, hard work of peacemaking could move forward.

(I have maintained the punctuation of the transcript prepared by CNN which is my source.) If I try to read the speech with an open mind, I am left with the distinct impression that this meeting resuscitated a peace process that was utterly moribund: 'they saw each other as human beings, and the slow, hard work of peacemaking could move forward.' One is left with the impression that Hillary Clinton's role in the success of the peace process in Northern Ireland was enormous. But note that she does not actually say this, in the technical sense of *say* that is involved in 'what is said'. Reread the crucial part of the passage: 'they saw each other as human beings, and the slow, hard work of peacemaking could move forward.' Let us assume for the moment that *they* refers to the participants in the meeting being described. The passage, then, just says that two things happened: first, that the participants in the meeting saw each other as human beings; and second, that the slow, hard work of peacemaking could move forward. It does not say that the slow, hard work of peacemaking could move forward *because* the participants in this one, comparatively small, meeting saw each other as human beings. But that is the conclusion that listeners may very well have drawn. Clinton, then, implicated that the peace process was revived because of her meeting. Again, this seems to be a relevance implicature: why would she be talking about the peace process moving forward, in what was evidently an attempt to advertise her foreign policy achievements, if she was not responsible for the peace process moving forward? And since she only implicated that she was responsible, she left herself plenty of room to manoeuvre in the event of anyone calling her on it: she never stated that she was solely responsible, lots of other people helped, and so on.

In fact this passage is more complex than I have so far indicated. As well as implicature, it also provides rather nice illustrations of ambiguities caused by implicit content and indexicality. To take the implicit content first, what exactly do you think is meant by the word *peacemaking* in the final part of the extract? My first impression, and I suspect most people's, is that Clinton was referring to the peace process as a whole, including the political negotiations that eventually led to the momentous Good Friday Agreement of 1998. She had, after all, mentioned 'the peace process in Northern Ireland' at the start of the quoted passage. But it would also be possible for Clinton to claim, if anyone accused her of deceit, that by *peacemaking* she meant 'peacemaking between the people gathered round the table in her meeting'; that would give rise to a very different proposition. And finally, turning to indexicality, who are we to take as the referent of *they* in 'they saw each other as human beings'? The most plausible solution in terms of what Clinton could have achieved with her one meeting is the people around the table, which is what I assumed above. But it would be eminently possible for someone caught up in the rhetoric to assume that *they* referred to the entire Protestant and Catholic population of Northern Ireland. This is especially so because Clinton twice used *they* to refer to the entire Protestant and Catholic population in an earlier part of the passage, repeated here:

(35) Because they don't go to school together, they don't live together and it was only in large measure because I really asked them to come that they were there...

In 'they don't go to school together, they don't live together', *they* seemingly refers to the entire population. This interpretation of the *they* in 'they saw each other as human beings' would nicely complement the interpretation of *peacemaking* whereby it refers to the Northern Ireland peace process as a whole.

The effects of context on what is said and what is conveyed are huge. And such effects frequently lay snares for the unwary.

8

Meaning and thought

Does the language we speak influence the way we think? Does it even render certain thoughts unthinkable? Or guide us inexorably towards certain others?

This view, sometimes in a very strong form, seems to have a certain currency. This is partly through its endorsement by various of the more fashionable philosophers and literary theorists. Ludwig Wittgenstein (1889–1951), for example, opined, 'The limits of my language mean the limits of my world.' The influence of the view can also be attributed to George Orwell's *Nineteen Eighty-Four*, in which totalitarian philologists employed by the Party have concocted Newspeak, a language which is supposed to make its speakers incapable of expressing or even entertaining any thought that deviates from the orthodoxy of Ingsoc (English Socialism). Here is how Orwell describes the language in the Appendix to his novel:

The purpose of Newspeak was not only to provide a medium of expression for the world-view and mental habits proper to the devotees of Ingsoc, but to make all other modes of thought impossible. It was intended that when Newspeak had been adopted once and for all and Oldspeak forgotten, a heretical thought—that is, a thought diverging from the principles of Ingsoc—should be literally unthinkable, at least so far as thought is dependent on words.

Although this is strong stuff, expressing a remarkable confidence in the ability of language to shape thought, it is worth noting the loophole 'at least so far as thought is dependent on words'. Orwell does not quite close the door to thought not being wholly dependent on words.

As well as Orwell, the potentially stultifying effects of our language are particularly associated with the names of the linguists Edward Sapir (1884–1939) and Benjamin Lee Whorf (1897–1941). Sapir was born in Germany but emigrated to the USA, where he taught anthropology at Yale; Whorf was American, by trade a fire inspector for an insurance company, but a talented linguist and a student of Sapir's. The two are associated with what is now called the *Sapir-Whorf hypothesis*, though they did not coin this term themselves. But what exactly was the hypothesis? Sapir and Whorf's writings on this matter tend to be vivid but vague, as the following quotation from Whorf illustrates:

We dissect nature along lines laid down by our native languages. The categories and types that we isolate from the world of phenomena we do not find there because they stare every observer in the face; on the contrary, the world is presented in a kaleidoscopic flux of impressions which has to be organized by our minds—and this means largely by the linguistic systems in our minds. We cut nature up, organize it into concepts, and ascribe significances as we do, largely because we are parties to an agreement to organize it in this way— an agreement that holds throughout our speech community and is codified in the patterns of our language. The agreement is, of course, an implicit and unstated one, *but its terms are absolutely obligatory*; we cannot talk at all except by subscribing to the organization and classification of data which the agreement decrees.

This is all very portentous. The basic thought seems to be that the only conceptual distinctions we can make are those encoded in our language; and that the reason for this is that our language imposes those distinctions on the sense data we take in from the world. But when we look more closely, we become unsure about what exactly is being claimed. We read that the kaleidoscopic flux of impressions with which we are buffeted is organized *largely* by the linguistic systems in our minds; that we cut nature up as we do *largely* because we are parties to a linguistically sustained agreement along those lines.

The exact reach of these largelys is not specified. Similar hedges can be found in Sapir's writing on the subject.

But we should not judge a view solely on the basis of people's unwillingness to express it. I will here present three versions of the Sapir-Whorf hypothesis, including a very strong one, based on Sapir and Whorf's own writings and on related work in the current technical literature:

(1) a. The strong Sapir-Whorf hypothesis. The only conceptual distinctions we can make are those encoded in our language; and the reason for this is that our language imposes those distinctions on our sense data (and we have no other source for such distinctions).

   b. The restricted Sapir-Whorf hypothesis. There are some topics such that the only conceptual distinctions we can make regarding them are those encoded in our language; and the reason for this is that our language imposes those distinctions on the relevant sense data (and we have no other source for such distinctions).

   c. The watered-down Sapir-Whorf hypothesis. There are some topics such that the way we habitually or stereotypically think about them is influenced by the language we speak.

The strong Sapir-Whorf hypothesis is based on the passage of Whorf quoted above, with the adverb *largely* removed. The restricted version keeps the idea that we are incapable of making conceptual distinctions that are not made in our language, but allows that this might hold only with respect to certain topics. And the watered-down version gives up on the central idea of the first two versions and allows that we might, after all, be able to make conceptual distinctions not provided by our language; but it maintains, nevertheless, that our language does have some less drastic influence on our thought, by influencing the way that we habitually or stereotypically think about some topics. If this last hypothesis is correct, we will naturally want to ask how many such topics there are and to what extent we are influenced in this way.

The strong Sapir-Whorf hypothesis, then, says that the only conceptual distinctions we can make are those encoded in our language. It is universally agreed among cognitive scientists that this hypothesis is false. For one thing, simple introspection can often tell people that they do have concepts of things that they do not have words for. The American psychologist Greg Murphy relates that he regularly asks students in his courses which of them have a name for those clumps of dust that accumulate under beds on wooden floors. He typically finds that about half the class does (with *dust bunnies* and *dust monsters* being popular choices) while half the class does not. But the ones who do not have names for these things do recognize what Murphy is talking about, and so they presumably have DUST BUNNY concepts without corresponding words. Relatedly, new words, with previously unexpressed meanings, are regularly coined. (As I write, there is some concern about possible damage to internet services caused by *hacktivists*, who seem to be people who engage in social activism by means of computer hacking.) If our thought is constrained to run in channels carved out by our language, it is mysterious how people are able to formulate new concepts in this way.

As if these objections were not enough, there is excellent evidence of conceptual distinctions made by individuals who do not have any language. Susan Schaller, an American sign language interpreter and teacher, tells the story of meeting Ildefonso, a 27-year-old Mexican immigrant in Los Angeles who was congenitally deaf and had never acquired any language, spoken or signed. But he was clearly able to make conceptual distinctions: he had worked successfully in a number of agricultural jobs, for one thing. Eventually, after much patient work by Schaller, Ildefonso was able to become fluent in American Sign Language. And finally, psychologist Karen Wynn, in an experiment published in 1992, showed that babies as young as five months (well before the acquisition of number terminology) can do some elementary counting. Babies were shown a Mickey Mouse doll until they became bored and their eyes wandered. Then a screen came up and someone reached behind it with another doll and placed it there. When the screen came down, if there were two dolls present (something the babies had not just seen) the babies looked for a few seconds and then were bored again: they plainly expected there to be two dolls behind the screen. But if there was just one doll (something that the babies had just been looking at) they were captivated: this evidently went counter to their expectations.

There is good reason to believe, then, that human beings can make conceptual distinctions that are not encoded by any languages they happen to speak.

What of the restricted Sapir-Whorf hypothesis? Recall that according to this view there are some topics such that the only conceptual distinctions we can make regarding them are those encoded in our language; and this comes about, as before, by our language imposing distinctions on the relevant sense data. This theory was also thought for a long time to be false. Recently, however, debate on it has been rekindled by some work on the recognition of numbers by the British psycholinguist Peter Gordon. In a 2004 article in the journal *Science*, Gordon reported that he had visited a remote hunter-gatherer tribe called the Pirahã, who live along the Maici River in the Lowland Amazonia region of Brazil. The Pirahã, of whom there are only about 250, are almost completely monolingual in their own language and have rejected assimilation into Brazilian society. Among other interesting properties, the Pirahã language has few or no number terms. The Pirahã words that look most like numbers are *hói* (with falling pitch), *hoí* (rising pitch) and *baagiso/aibaagi*. It is initially tempting to see these three words as forming a 'one-two-many' system of a type that has been documented in other languages: *hói* is often used for one object, *hoí* for two objects, and *baagiso* or *aibaagi* for more than that. But Gordon observed that 'whereas the word for "two" always denoted a larger quantity than the word for "one" (when used in the same context), the word for "one" was sometimes used to denote just a small quantity such as two or three or sometimes more.' A later study by Michael Frank, Daniel Everett, Evelina Fedorenko, and Edward Gibson found that *hói* was used for quantities of one to six, *hoí* for quantities of two to ten, and *baagiso* or *aibaagi* for quantities of three to ten. (They did not try to go above ten.) They suggest that *hói* means something like 'few' rather than 'one' or even 'roughly one'.

It seems, then, that the Pirahã do not have words for numbers. They certainly do not have words for numbers above two. Gordon wanted to find out if, in spite of not having words for numbers above two, the Pirahã could nevertheless make distinctions between such numbers. He conducted several experiments to find out.

In one task, Gordon put some candy in a box with a small number of pictures of fish on the lid. There might be three fish on the lid, for example. He would then put the box behind his back and bring out two boxes: the original and another one identical except for the fact that it bore one fish more or less. He would ask his informants to pick out the box with the candy in it. When the task involved telling the difference between three and four fish, performance was just below 50%, i.e. around chance level. In another task, informants were asked to look at a small group of nuts for about eight seconds. Gordon then dropped the nuts into an opaque can into which the informants could not see. He withdrew them one at a time; and after each nut was taken out, informants were asked if there were any nuts left in the can. When two nuts had been placed in the can, the Pirahã correctly identified the moment when the can became empty about 90% of the time; when there were three nuts, they did so about 65% of the time; with four nuts, the figure was about 60%; with five, about 35%; and with six, about 10%.

So the answer Gordon arrived at was negative. The Pirahã could not reliably tell the difference between three and four, four and five, and so on. He concludes, 'The results of these studies show that the Pirahãs' impoverished counting system limits their ability to enumerate exact quantities when set sizes exceed two or three items.'

On the face of it, this is a classic Whorfian conclusion and strong support for the restricted Sapir-Whorf hypothesis. Number would be a topic such that the only conceptual distinctions we can make regarding it are those encoded in our language; since the Pirahã do not have any conceptual distinctions about number encoded in their language, except words for 'few' and 'many', they cannot make any conceptual distinctions about number, except distinctions along the lines of 'few' and 'many'.

But it is worth asking how we can be sure about the direction of causation in this case. Remember that Whorf's idea, as expressed in my strong and restricted versions of the Sapir-Whorf hypothesis, was that our language imposes a set of distinctions on our thought. But what if our thought was constrained for some other reason? If there was some other reason why we could not (or would not) grasp a particular concept, it is natural to assume that our language would not have a word for that concept. Why would we have a word for something about which we had no idea? So it seems that the door is open for a sceptical alternative hypothesis: the Pirahã are unable (or unwilling) to think about numbers, and that is the reason their language does not have any words for numbers. The chain of causality goes from thought to language, in other words, and not vice versa.

This is certainly the line taken by the outside world's greatest expert on Pirahã language and culture, the American linguist Daniel Everett. Everett's own story is a remarkable one. He and his wife Keren first went to the Pirahã as Christian missionaries in 1977 and returned regularly at intervals for over twenty years. Previous attempts to evangelize this people had foundered due to the difficulty of their language and the lack of interest in outside cultures they displayed. The Everetts battled snakes, malaria, and occasional homicidal villagers in order to learn the Pirahã language and communicate God's word. Eventually Daniel Everett produced a translation of the Gospel of Mark into Pirahã and distributed recordings of it in hand-cranked cassette players. All to no avail. In fact, as Everett relates in his gripping book *Don't sleep, there are snakes*, the Pirahãs' pragmatic and sceptical attitude towards tales of old-time religion eventually played a large part in converting him: by the late 1980s he was an atheist.

Everett's take on the Pirahãs' inability to count is as follows. He claims that Pirahã culture is governed by a constraint called the *immediacy of experience principle*:

(2) Declarative Pirahã utterances contain only assertions directly related to the moment of speech, either experienced by the speaker or as witnessed by someone alive during the lifetime of the speaker.

This principle, if it obtains, would certainly seem to explain other interesting features of Pirahã language and culture noted by Everett: the fact that they have no creation myths and no attested stories of historical events that took place more than a generation or two ago. It is less clear, however, how it is supposed to explain the absence of numbers or the Pirahãs' inability to count. According to Everett, the connection is supposed to be that counting 'entails abstract generalizations that range in principle beyond immediate experience'. I think more would have to be said in order to make this explanation work. In principle, counting can of course involve abstract generalizations that range beyond immediate experience. ('Every Platonic Form is instantiated by twelve ancient megaliths on the dark side of the moon.') But it does not have to. A sincere utterance of 'Help, my left leg is being devoured by three panthers!' is rather directly related to the moment of speech as experienced by the speaker. So the immediacy of experience principle should not prohibit it, nor any one of an indefinitely large number of sentences involving numbers and immediate experience.

One could equally well argue about any word whatsoever that, since it could be used in an abstract generalization that ranges beyond immediate experience, it should therefore not be allowed in Pirahã. But Pirahã is not wholly devoid of words.

A more plausible alternative hypothesis has been advanced by the linguists Andew Nevins, David Pesetsky, and Cilene Rodrigues. They point out that there is a correlation between hunter-gatherer subsistence and restricted numeral systems. This makes sense, because such societies have no commerce or complex administration of a kind that would stimulate the invention of larger ones. So the Pirahã language has no numbers, according to this hypothesis, because the Pirahã people, given their culture, have no need of number concepts. Again, the direction of causality is reversed from that alleged by

Gordon. The Pirahã having no number concepts would, of course, explain their performance in Gordon's experiments.

It should be noted that this alternative hypothesis does not actually rule out the possibility that the direction of causality runs as Gordon alleged. We are simply left with two alternatives. But there is a certain naturalness in the alternative hypothesis that could well be thought to recommend it. So the restricted Sapir-Whorf hypothesis, at least as viewed in the light of Gordon's study, should be regarded as not proven.

What of the watered-down Sapir-Whorf hypothesis? Recall that this states that there are some topics such that the way we habitually or stereotypically think about them is influenced by the language we speak. This seems to be correct, although it should be emphasized that the degree to which we are influenced in this way may not be very great. Some of the best evidence in support of the watered-down Sapir-Whorf hypothesis comes from the work of the Russian psychologist Lera Boroditsky and her colleagues.

The experiments of Boroditsky's that I will review deal with grammatical gender. Languages that divide their nouns into masculine and feminine (and those that add neuter) frequently attribute masculine gender to nouns that name things that are biologically male and feminine to those that stand for the biological females. (Occasional exceptions are observed, of course.) Other nouns are divided up seemingly randomly, as Mark Twain observed in his wonderful essay 'The awful German language':

[A] tree is male, its buds are female, its leaves are neuter; horses are sexless, dogs are male, cats are female,—Tom-cats included, of course...a person's nose, lips, shoulders, breast, hands, hips, and toes are of the female sex; and his hair, ears, eyes, chin, legs, knees, heart, and conscience, haven't any sex at all. The inventor of the language probably got what he knew about a conscience from hearsay.

Boroditsky wondered whether the masculine and feminine gender of the nouns that designated things that were not biologically male or female had any effect on how people thought about the things in question. Anecdotal evidence indicated that there might be an effect here. Here is an extract from Andrei Makine's novel *Dreams of My Russian Summers*, as translated by Geoffrey Strachan. The protagonist is Russian, and his grandmother Charlotte is French:

As a child I had absorbed all the sounds of Charlotte's language. I swam in them, without wondering why that glint in the grass, that colored, scented, living brilliance, sometimes existed in the masculine and had a crunchy, fragile, crystalline identity, imposed, it seemed, by one of its names, tsvetok; and was sometimes enveloped in a velvety, feltlike, and feminine aura, becoming une fleur.

The Russian word for 'flower', *tsvetok*, is masculine, whereas the French word, *fleur* is feminine.

Is it only sensitive young novelists learning French from their grandmothers who feel this kind of thing, or is the effect more general? Lera Boroditsky, Lauren Schmidt, and Webb Phillips, in a study published in 2003, performed two experiments to find out. Firstly, they investigated the effect of grammatical gender on memory. They used German and Spanish, two languages with grammatical gender which are such that many common object-names have one gender in German and a different one in Spanish, as with the example of 'flower' in French and Russian. For example, the word for 'apple' is masculine in German (*der Apfel*) and feminine in Spanish (*la manzana*).

The experimenters assembled twenty-four English nouns naming inanimate objects for which the corresponding nouns in Spanish and German had inconsistent genders. The subjects in the experiment were native speakers of Spanish and German. Both groups were competent in English, and the experiment was conducted in English. The experimenters taught each subject personal names for each object. For example an apple might be called Patrick or Patricia. For any given object, some speakers of German would be told a male name for it and some a female name; and likewise for the Spanish speakers. So some Spanish speakers had to memorize a male name like Patrick for the apple, while other Spanish speakers had to memorize a female name; and likewise for the German speakers.

The subjects were then tested on how well they remembered the personal names given to the objects. The result was that when a speaker had been given a name for an object that was of the same gender as the word for that kind of object in their native language, they were better at remembering the name. When the name was inconsistent in gender with the word in their native language, they were worse at remembering it than in the other case. For example, German speakers were better at remembering a male name like Patrick for an apple than they were at remembering a female name like Patricia. Conversely, Spanish speakers were better at remembering female names for apples than they were male names.

Why might this have happened? Boroditsky and her colleagues suggest that children learning a language that has grammatical gender have no reason to suppose that masculine and feminine genders of nouns do not reflect some real properties of the objects concerned, especially when they see biological males lining up with the masculine gender and biological females with the feminine. So, perhaps in an effort to remember the genders of the different nouns, children start focussing on stereotypically masculine qualities of objects named by masculine nouns and on stereotypically feminine qualities of objects named by feminine nouns. The result is that the conceptual representations that are the meanings of words (according to psychologists and Chomskyan linguists) are actually affected: the objects are portrayed, as it were, as having masculine or feminine properties. And according to contemporary psychology, there is no set of general-purpose conceptual representations that are somehow separate from the ones involved in word meaning. The concept APPLE that is the meaning of the word *apple* just is our concept of apples, with no back-ups or alternatives in sight. So learning a language with grammatical gender can affect your concepts. And with their concepts in this condition, it is small wonder that the Spanish-speaking and German-speaking subjects behaved as they did: they found it harder to remember names that disagreed in gender with the conceptual representations of the things they were names for.

In case you are wondering how, in concrete terms, one might go about portraying inanimate objects as masculine or feminine, here is an example: Boroditsky and her colleagues suggest that a toaster might be portrayed with an emphasis on its hard, metallic, and technological aspects in the minds of people for whom the corresponding word is masculine; but with an emphasis on its domestic and nourishing properties in the case of a feminine word.

Now this might be starting to sound like an awful lot of weight to put on one memory test, so Boroditsky and her colleagues tried to probe more directly to see what characteristics are associated with various objects by Spanish- and German-speakers. Using the list of 24 objects from the previous experiment, they asked Spanish- and German-speakers to write down the first three adjectives that came into their minds to describe each object on the list. After all the results were in, a group of English-speakers was asked to rate all the adjectives used according to whether they portrayed a masculine or a feminine quality. The results were that subjects produced adjectives that were rated more masculine for nouns that were masculine in their language, and more feminine for nouns that were feminine in their language.

Some of the examples were extremely striking. The word for 'key' is masculine in German (*der Schlüssel*) and feminine in Spanish (*la llave*). German-speakers used adjectives like *hard, heavy, jagged, metal, serrated*, and *useful*. Spanish-speakers used adjectives like *golden, intricate, little, lovely, shiny*, and *tiny*. The word for 'bridge' is feminine in German (*die Brücke*), masculine in Spanish (*el puente*). German-speakers used adjectives like *beautiful, elegant, fragile, peaceful, pretty*, and *slender*. Spanish-speakers (and you might like to imagine a deep manly voice at this point) used adjectives like *big, dangerous, long, strong, sturdy*, and *towering*. This, then, was a spectacular result.

Nevertheless, one might conceivably argue against the Whorfian force of these results by alleging that the direction of causation runs the other way, as with the Pirahã case. Perhaps some previously unremarked features of German and Hispanophone culture lead the relevant people to regard bridges as having feminine and masculine traits, respectively, and the respective languages spoken in these cultures merely reflect this. It is entirely unclear what these cultural features could be; but to lay such doubts to rest, Boroditsky and her colleagues decided to invent a language that had a gender distinction and have people learn it. Since there was no culture attached to this particular language, culture could not be held responsible for any effects that were observed.

Boroditsky, Schmidt, and Phillips taught native English-speakers elements of a fictional language called Gumbuzi. The subjects were told that Gumbuzi nouns were divided into two classes called *oosative* and *soupative*. There were two words for 'the', *oos* or *sou*, and which one was used with which noun had to be memorized. (It can be seen that this is exactly how some languages with gender systems behave: compare German *der* vs *die* for 'the', and Spanish *el* vs *la*.) Nouns denoting male people and female people always clustered together, although the class they were said to belong to differed between subjects, so that one subject might learn that girls and women were oosative and men and boys were soupative, while another learnt the opposite. As with natural language gender systems, the categories extended to other objects too, so that one subject might learn that pans, forks, pencils, ballerinas, and girls were soupative while pots, spoons, pens, giants, and boys were oosative. Another, again, might learn the converse. The subjects were instructed in the distinction by means of labelled pictures on a computer screen (the picture of the giant clearly featuring a male giant) and were tested on twenty items until they could correctly tell for each one whether it was oosative or soupative.

When the subjects had learnt the distinction, they were shown the pictures again, without labels, and asked to come up with adjectives to describe them, as in the second experiment on Spanish- and German-speakers. As before, the adjectives were rated by an independent group as to whether they designated stereotypically male or stereotypically female characteristics.

As predicted, the subjects described inanimate objects that were grouped with biological females in the version of the gender system they had learnt in terms that were more stereotypically feminine than the ones used for the objects that were grouped with the biological males. Once again, some of the differences were quite striking. When a violin was assigned feminine gender in the test, it was described as *artsy, beautiful, creative, curvy, delicate, elegant, interesting, pretty,* and *wooden.* When it was grouped with the biological males, it was described as *chirping, difficult, impressive, noisy, overused, piercing, shiny, slender, voluptuous,* and *wooden.* Someone's attention evidently wandered there in producing *slender* and *voluptuous,* but that is the price one pays for using human beings in one's experiments.

So even when a gender system is one that was made up specially for an experiment, with no accompanying culture in sight, it influences how people think of the things whose names are assigned to the various genders.

In other work, Boroditsky has demonstrated similar effects stemming from other parts of language. In a 2001 publication, for example, she demonstrated that Mandarin-speakers and English-speakers have different conceptions of time, arguably deriving from the spatial metaphors that are used about time in their respective languages. In English, we tend to use horizontal metaphors: next week's faculty board meeting is looming ominously *ahead* of us, whereas last week's is safely *behind* us, and so on. In Mandarin, although horizontal metaphors for time are common, it is also common to use vertical metaphors: earlier events are said to be *shàng* 'up', while later ones are said to be *xià* 'down'. Boroditsky showed native Mandarin- and English-speakers pictures showing spatial relationships and asked questions about them. For example, there might be a picture of a black ball above a white ball and the subjects would have to say whether or not the white ball was below the black one; and similarly for pictures showing horizontal spatial relationships. The subjects were then asked questions about time, like 'Does March come earlier than April?' The length of time the subjects took to answer was measured with a computer. The two groups responded very differently. The English-speakers responded more quickly to the temporal questions when they were preceded by a question about horizontal spatial relationships, whereas the

Mandarin-speakers were quicker when they had just answered a question about vertical spatial relationships. Boroditsky explained the difference in terms of priming, or the activation of certain mental representations, a term that you may remember from the description of Pylkkänen's experiment in Chapter 3: working out the answer to a question about horizontal or vertical spatial relationships made the subjects more ready to think in those terms; the fact that this had an effect on their ability to think about time shows that people's mental representations of time are the same as or similar to their mental representations of space, as the use of spatial metaphors for time suggests; and the fact that Mandarin-speakers were primed by vertical spatial relations and English-speakers by horizontal ones shows that the two groups represent time differently. Why should they do this? Well, one group has been brought up speaking a language that commonly uses vertical spatial metaphors for time, and the other group has been brought up with only horizontal spatial metaphors for time. Interestingly, a group of native English-speakers who were trained to speak about time vertically (with sentences like *Monday is above Tuesday*) produced results very like those of the Mandarin-speakers when they were tested immediately after training.

To what extent, then, does the language we speak influence the way we think? The strong Sapir-Whorf hypothesis is unequivocally false. The restricted Sapir-Whorf hypothesis is not proven. The only version of the hypothesis that has been shown to have something going for it is the watered-down one.

And here, although the results from Boroditsky's experiments are fascinating and impressive as far as they go, it is important to bear in mind that we are in general talking about exceedingly small differences that would not be noticed if they were not probed experimentally. Take the memory test featuring apples named Patrick. When the subjects were remembering a name that was consistent with the object's gender according to their native language, their success rate was 86%; when the name was inconsistent with the object's gender in their native language, their success rate was 78%. The difference was statistically significant, but not exactly indicative of a drastic loss of mental capacity. In the experiment on Mandarin-

and English-speakers' representations of time, the differences that showed up were a matter of milliseconds: Mandarin-speakers took an average of 2.347 seconds to answer the temporal questions after vertical priming, for example, and 2.503 seconds to answer them after horizontal priming, a difference of 156 milliseconds. Again, this was statistically significant in the context of the experiment, but it is not something that anyone would ever notice in real life.

The different rosters of adjectives provided by the Spanish- and German-speakers for keys and bridges constitute perhaps the most dramatic result we have surveyed. But here too it is important to bear in mind the limitations of the finding. At most, it shows that the ways in which these two groups of people habitually think about bridges (and so on) is influenced by their native language. But no-one is claiming that German-speakers, for example, are incapable of appreciating that bridges can be long, strong, sturdy, and towering. And, as cognitive scientist Steven Pinker has remarked in this context, 'just because a German thinks a bridge is feminine, doesn't mean he's going to ask one out on a date.'

The currently available evidence, then, suggests that the language we speak influences the way we think only with respect to scarcely perceptible cognitive biases that can be measured only in milliseconds and subtle stereotypes that vanish instantly upon reflection.

9
Conclusion

For the record, and drawing on the preceding chapters, here is what I personally believe about meaning. Meanings are concepts. They reside inside people's heads, as part of words. We use words and their meanings in order to refer to things in the world or spin outlandish counterfactual tales that do not characterize our world (or any world—there is only one world). Your meaning for your word *chair* and my meaning for my word *chair* are distinct objects, although they are likely to be qualitatively very similar. They are unlikely to be qualitatively identical, however, meaning that there might be objects that you would call chairs and I would not, or vice versa. They are also likely to change over time inside us, even after we have reached maturity (or as much maturity as we are ever going to acquire). None of this matters very much for everyday usage, since the range of cases where we would agree that the word *chair* is appropriate is very large, and any differences between us might be discernible only by means of weird science fiction scenarios, psychological experiments, or both. But there are some practical repercussions: if a local ordinance says 'No vehicles in the park' and you are arrested for cycling in the park, it matters very much whether judge and jury think that bicycles are vehicles. Since meanings are part of our heads, it comes as no surprise that some aspects of their behaviour can be described quite well by mathematical models, in the same way that mathematics is used in other attempts to describe the physical world. But we should not believe in the literal existence of all the things (such as possible worlds) that figure in these mathematical models and sound like they cannot be in our heads. We should also not get carried away with our few successes along these lines. We have much to be modest about.

I hope that enough has been said in this book for these positions to sound, if not like true justified belief, then at least like justified belief. But it has not been my purpose to evangelize on behalf of a particular set of views, although I have made no sustained effort to conceal my opinions. I have rather been trying to show something of the intellectual excitement that runs through the study of meaning, excitement that arises from the pervasive controversy that characterizes the field and from the sense that this endeavour is fundamental to understanding ourselves as human beings. Another source of this intellectual excitement is the extraordinarily wide range of subjects that the study of meaning either touches on or crucially involves: one can become interested in a semantic question and not know whether the solution of it will lead one into the philosophy of language, metaphysics, linguistics, psychology, or neuroscience. It is quite likely to involve more than one discipline and very likely not to be definitively settled.

Sources and further reading

In the following notes, I give the main sources on which I have drawn and try to indicate how accessible they would be for someone just starting out on the study of semantics and related areas.

Chapter 1

In Plato's *Meno*, the definition of *knowledge* as something like 'true, justified belief' comes in section 98a. A lively and accessible introduction to truth, including the anti-sceptical manoeuvre mentioned in the text, is to be found in Simon Blackburn's *Truth: a Guide for the Perplexed* (Allen Lane, 2005). As for postmodernism, the Sokal hoax should have taught people everything they needed to know: see Alan Sokal's lucid and important *Beyond the Hoax: Science, Philosophy and Culture* (Oxford University Press, 2008), especially the first seven chapters. For a briefer assessment ('counterfeit philosophy'), you might like to try Anthony Kenny's excellent and highly readable *A New History of Western Philosophy*, volume 4, *Philosophy in the Modern World* (Oxford University Press, 2007), pages 90–96. Edmund Gettier's famous paper was published in the philosophical journal *Analysis* 23 (1963): 121–123. It will be mostly accessible to someone who has read the present book.

Noam Chomsky's discussion of *water*, *thing*, and other interesting words is to be found in Chapter 5 of his book *New Horizons in the Study of Language and Mind* (Cambridge University Press, 2000). The whole volume is a fascinating meditation on the nature of language and mind; while it might be tough going in places, much of it (especially Chapter 1) should be accessible to someone who has read the present book.

The lecture on metals by Robert Pond, 'Fun in metals', was published in the April 1987 edition of *Johns Hopkins Magazine*, pages 60–68. But I came across it in Chapter 2 of *The Big Book of Concepts* by Gregory Murphy (MIT Press, 2002), where it is used to make a point very similar to the one that I use it to illustrate. *The Big Book of Concepts* is a lucid and engaging introductory textbook on psychological research into concepts. I will refer to it again in connection with the next chapter.

The discussion of *gold* is based closely on the corresponding discussion in Lecture III of Saul Kripke's classic *Naming and Necessity* (Harvard University

Press, 1980). Although admirably clear and lively for a text in analytic philosophy, this is an advanced work that requires a fair amount of philosophical training to understand. The use of an evil demon for philosophical thought experiments goes back at least to the *Meditations* of Descartes.

The definition of *prime* in the text is based closely on the one in *What is Mathematics? An Elementary Approach to Ideas and Methods* by Richard Courant, Herbert Robbins, and Ian Stewart (Oxford University Press, 2nd edition, 1996), page 22.

Chapter 2

Russell set out his theory of propositions in Chapter IV of his book *The Principles of Mathematics* (Cambridge University Press, 1903). Again, this is not for beginners.

My discussion of abstract objects is influenced by the admirable summary given by Gideon Rosen in his article 'Abstract Objects' in the online Stanford Encyclopedia of Philosophy (http://plato.stanford.edu/entries/abstract-objects/). This article should be mostly accessible to someone who has read the current book. In general, the Stanford Encyclopedia of Philosophy (SEP) is extremely reliable and an excellent resource. If you would like to find out more about some of the other philosophical topics broached in the current chapter, you would be well advised to look at the SEP articles on Nominalism (Gonzalo Rodriguez-Pereyra), Platonism in Metaphysics (Mark Balaguer), and Properties (Chris Swoyer).

For allegations of the existence of Santa Claus, see Nathan Salmon, 'Nonexistence', *Nous* 32 (1998): 277–399; and Scott Soames *Beyond Rigidity: the Unfinished Semantic Agenda of* Naming and Necessity (Oxford University Press, 2002), pages 93–95. These works are aimed at professional philosophers.

The Aristotelian quotation is from *De interpretatione* 16a3–4 (my translation). The extract from John Buridan is from *Summulae de dialectica* 4.1.2, in the translation of Gyula Klima, *John Buridan: Summulae de dialectica* (Yale University Press, 2001). Locke's dictum comes from Book III, Chapter II, section 2 of *An Essay Concerning Human Understanding*. Mill's reply, quoted a little later, comes from Chapter II of *A System of Logic*. The works by Locke and Mill are pretty accessible, provided that you can deal with seventeenth-century English in the case of Locke.

Chomsky's views on language in general have been set out in many places; as well as *New Horizons in the Study of Language and Mind*, cited above, a good starting point would be his *Knowledge of Language: Its Nature, Origin, and Use* (Praeger, 1986), the first two chapters of which should be fairly accessible for someone who has read the present book. The quotation about rocks and hands is from *New Horizons*, page 150. Examples like the one involving *Jeeves and the Feudal Spirit* can be found on pages 180-1 of *New Horizons* and on page 236 of Chomsky's *The Minimalist Program* (MIT Press, 1995). Under no circumstances should any beginner in the field attempt to read *The Minimalist Program*.

The version of the prototype view that I describe was proposed by James Hampton, 'Polymorphous concepts in semantic memory', *Journal of Verbal Learning and Verbal Behavior* 18 (1979), 441-61. It is based on Eleanor Rosch and Carolyn B. Mervis, 'Family resemblance: studies in the internal structure of categories', *Cognitive Psychology* 7, 573-605. These articles are rather technical. An accessible overview can be obtained from Gregory Murphy's *Big Book of Concepts*, cited above, especially Chapters 1-3 and Chapter 11. For Fodor's treatment of the *pet fish* problem, see his book *Concepts: where cognitive science went wrong* (Clarendon Press, 1998), pages 102-7. This work is hard going in places, but much of it should be accessible to someone who has read the present book. An excellent and generally accessible survey of theories of concepts and their problems can be found in 'Concepts and cognitive science', by Stephen Laurence and Eric Margolis, Chapter 1 of *Concepts: core readings*, an anthology edited by the same authors in reverse order (Margolis and Laurence—MIT Press, 1999).

Frege alleges the incompatibility of the internalist theory of meaning and successful communication in his essay 'Der Gedanke: eine logische Untersuchung', *Beiträge zur Philosophie des deutschen Idealismus* 2 (1918-19), 58-77. An English translation, 'The thought: a logical inquiry', by A.M. and Marcelle Quinton, can be found in the periodical *Mind* 65 (1956), 289-311. It should be largely accessible for someone who has read the present book.

I got the *jejune* example from page 87 of William Lycan's *Philosophy of language: a contemporary introduction* (Routledge, second edition, 2008). This is a lively, sound, accessible, and generally excellent textbook that often takes a significantly different view from the current book and could therefore be a useful corrective.

McCloskey and Glucksberg's article is called 'Natural categories: well-defined or fuzzy sets?' and appears in the journal *Memory & Cognition* 6 (1978), 467-72. It is aimed at professional psychologists.

Chapter 3

The terms *U* (upper class) and *non-U* were introduced by the British linguist Alan Ross (1907–1980) in his essay 'Linguistic class-indicators in present-day English' in the journal *Neuphilologische Mitteilungen* 55 (1954), 113–49. The terms were subsequently popularized by Nancy Mitford. See her book *Noblesse Oblige: An Inquiry into the Identifiable Characteristics of the English Aristocracy* (Hamish Hamilton, 1956).

The vagueness of the word *bald* and similar terms was apparently first noted by Eubulides of Miletus (fourth century BC). Baldness was one of his examples, as was the *sorites* ('heaper') paradox: if you have a heap of wheat and remove one grain, is it still a heap? And if you remove another one? And another? Do two grains of wheat make a heap? An excellent and generally accessible historical and theoretical discussion of this topic can be found in *Vagueness* (Routledge, 1994) by the Oxford philosopher Timothy Williamson.

The paper by Pylkkänen, Llinás, and Murphy is 'The representation of polysemy: MEG evidence', *Journal of Cognitive Neuroscience* 18 (2006), 1–13. The link between the M350 and lexical activation was established by Liina Pylkkänen, Andrew Stringfellow, and Alec Marantz, 'Neuromagnetic evidence for the timing of lexical activation: an MEG component sensitive to phonotactic probability but not to neighborhood density', *Brain and Language* 81 (2002), 666–78. These rather technical papers are aimed strictly at neuroscientists.

Chapter 4

Stephen Schiffer gives the argument about life on Venus, and some related ones, on pages 12–14 of his book *The Things We Mean* (Oxford University Press, 2003). Chomsky's example of the bank burning down and moving across the street is on page 180 of his *New Horizons in the Study of Language and Mind*. A criticism of Schiffer's argument (and similar ones) similar in spirit to mine can be found in the essay 'There are no abstract objects' by the Oxford philosopher Cian Dorr; it can be found in *Contemporary Debates in Metaphysics*, edited by Theodore Sider, John Hawthorne, and Dean Zimmerman (Blackwell, 2008), pages 32–63. The first section of the essay, which is the relevant one, should be accessible to someone who has read the current book; the paper becomes steadily more difficult after that point.

My exposition of Duns Scotus's version of possible worlds is adapted from the one in Anthony Kenny's *A New History of Western Philosophy*, volume 2, *Medieval Philosophy* (Oxford University Press, 2005), pages 202, 244–5. Leibniz wrote his thoughts on the best of all possible worlds in his *Discourse on Metaphysics* (1685) and *Essays in Theodicy* (1710). My account is influenced by Kenny's descriptions in volume 3 of his history, *The Rise of Modern Philosophy* (Oxford University Press, 2006), pages 72–4, 313–14; and also by the relevant articles in the online Stanford Encyclopedia of Philosophy ('Gottfried Wilhelm Leibniz' by Brandon Look, 'Leibniz's modal metaphysics' by the same author, and 'Leibniz on the problem of evil' by Michael Murray). The passage from Leibniz's letter to Arnauld is to be found on page 49 of *The Leibniz–Arnauld Correspondence*, edited and translated by H.T. Mason (Manchester University Press, 1967).

David Lewis set out his theory of possible worlds in his book *On the Plurality of Worlds* (Blackwell, 1986). The quotation about maximal mereological sums is from page 73 and the incredulous stares feature on page 133. This book is unusually limpid for a research monograph in philosophy and could possibly be tackled by someone who has read the present book, although the going would be rough in places. A good and accessible summary of the doctrine of modal realism is to be found in 'Concrete possible worlds' by Phillip Bricker, in the volume *Contemporary Debates in Metaphysics*, cited above, pages 111–34. The following essay in the same book (pages 135–51), 'Ersatz possible worlds' by Joseph Melia, offers a good survey of the variety of ersatz worlds available but would be slightly more difficult for a beginner.

Davidson's seminal article on truth and meaning is 'Truth and meaning', *Synthese* 17 (1967), 304–23. Lewis sets out a brief version of the argument that truth conditions are possible worlds on page 22 of his article 'General semantics', *Synthese* 22 (1970), 18–67. Stalnaker does the same in his article 'Pragmatics' in *Synthese* 22 (1970), 272–89. These works are rather technical.

Barwise and Perry's main work on situations is *Situations and Attitudes* (2nd edition, CSLI Publications, 1999; originally published by MIT Press in 1983). Strictly speaking, Barwise and Perry do not say that sentence meanings are sets of situations, since they quite rightly maintain that sentence meanings must interact with the situations in which sentences are spoken, in order to make indexicals refer to the right things (e.g. in order to make the word *I* pick out the current speaker). This complicates matters. But their proposal is close to what I describe in the text. See page 19 of their book, which is, however, dense, technical, and aimed strictly at philosophers and theoretical linguists. A useful modern resource is Angelika Kratzer's article

'Situations in natural language semantics' in the Stanford Encyclopedia of Philosophy; this again, however, is not for beginners.

The advisibility of using impossible situations is urged by Barwise and Perry on page 96 of *Situations and Individuals*.

Eugene Wigner's article 'The unreasonable effectiveness of mathematics in the natural sciences' appeared in *Communications on Pure and Applied Mathematics* 13(1): 1–14, 1960.

William Ladusaw set out his landmark theory of NPI-licensing in his article 'On the notion "affective" in the analysis of negative polarity items', *Journal of Linguistic Research* 1: 1–16, 1980. This technical article is aimed at theoretical linguists.

The classic reference for the modularity of mind is Jerry Fodor's book *The Modularity of Mind* (MIT Press, 1983). This, again, is somewhat technical.

Chapter 5

My source for the history of the wife beating example is a learned footnote on page 119 of Laurence Horn's essay 'Pragmatic theory', in *Linguistic Theory: Foundations* (Cambridge University Press, 1988), edited by Frederick Newmeyer, pages 113–145. I do not know when the version with wives was introduced. The earliest written source I have found for it dates from 1961: page 127 of H.P. Grice's essay 'The causal theory of perception' in *Proceedings of the Aristotelian Society*, Supplementary volume 35, pages 121–152. (Here, incidentally, the example is *Smith has left off beating his wife.*) But in the subsequent discussion, Grice already refers to this as 'a stock case'.

The piece about Arlen Specter and the definite article is 'The crushing of Arlen Specter', on page 54 of *The Economist* volume 395, number 8683, May 22–28, 2010. Frege's remarks on *the* are to be found in his seminal essay 'Über Sinn und Bedeutung' in *Zeitschrift für Philosophie und Philosophische Kritik* 100, 25–50, 1892 (frequently translated and anthologized as 'On sense and reference'). Russell's influential paper on this topic is 'On denoting', *Mind* 14: 479–93, 1905; and Strawson's is 'On referring', *Mind* 59: 320–44, 1950. Lasersohn's paper is 'Existence presuppositions and background knowledge' in *Journal of Semantics* 10: 112–22, 1993; and von Fintel's is 'Would you believe it? The King of France is back! (Presuppositions and truth-value intuitions)', in *Descriptions and Beyond* (Oxford University Press, 2004), edited by Marga Reimer and Anne Bezuidenhout, pages 315–41. None of these articles (except the *Economist* one, of course) would be particularly accessible to beginners in semantics. For a more comprehensible treatment of definite descriptions, readers might like to try Stephen Neale's modern classic *Descriptions* (MIT Press, 1990), which gives a lot of sound background information in a lively manner while presenting many influential innovations. (Neale is more sympathetic to Russell than I would be, however.)

The examples about the block in the box on the table come from Kenneth Church and Ramesh Patil's article 'Coping with syntactic ambiguity or how to put the block in the box on the table', *American Journal of Computational Linguistics* 8(3–4): 139–49, 1982. This article presupposes a fair acquaintance with linguistics and theoretical computer science.

My introduction to quantifier phrases was influenced (Lewis Carroll and all) by the treatment given on pages 130–7 of *Meaning and Argument. An introduction to logic through language* (Wiley-Blackwell, 2009, 2nd edition), by Ernest Lepore with Sam Cumming. This is an excellent logic textbook that pays a lot of attention to the meaning and formalization of a broad range of natural language phenomena. It could very well form the next port of call for the reader of the current book who is interested in the more formal side of things.

The example *Exactly half the boys kissed some girl* is quite well known in the field. It originated on page 11 of Eddy Ruys's PhD dissertation, *The Scope of Indefinites* (Utrecht University). The whole of my discussion of this example and *Every man loves some woman* is heavily influenced by the first chapter of this dissertation.

The idea of Logical Forms comes from Chomsky's essay 'Conditions on rules of grammar', *Linguistic Analysis* 2, 303–51, 1976. The rule of Quantifier Raising, as described here, was developed by Robert May's (1977) MIT PhD dissertation *The Grammar of Quantification*. These works require a good knowledge of syntactic theory for profitable reading.

The theory of Barker and Shan described here appears in their article 'Donkey anaphora is in-scope binding', *Semantics and Pragmatics* 1(1): 1–46, 2008 (doi: 10.3765/sp.1.1). This article is rather technical.

My account of the Casement trial is taken from the official transcription of the proceedings, 1 *Rex* v. *Sir Roger David Casement* 1916. The trial record can also be found at *Rex* v. *Casement* [1917] 1 K.B. 98. In the pagination of the former version, the defence's interpretation of the relevant part of the Treason Act can be found on pages 121–2, and the prosecution's can be found on page 137. The relevant section of statute is the Treason Act, 1351, 25 Edw. 3, c. 2.

Chapter 6

Frege expounded his doctrine that semantic compositionality was functional application in his essay 'Function and concept' (originally 'Funktion und Begriff', 1891), pages 21–41 of *Translations from the Philosophical Writings of Gottlob Frege* (Blackwell, 1960), by Max Black and Peter Geach.

An excellent introduction to compositional semantics is *Semantics in Generative Grammar* (Blackwell, 1998), by Irene Heim and Angelika Kratzer. It assumes more syntactic theory than I have described here; but other than that nothing is assumed that would not be within the ken of the reader of the present book.

Chapter 7

David Kaplan's classic paper about indexicals is called 'Demonstratives'. It was finished in 1977 and circulated for several years in manuscript form. So influential was it in this format that there seemed little need to publish it formally. It eventually saw formal publication in a book devoted to discussing it: pages 481–563 of *Themes from Kaplan* (Oxford University Press, 1989), edited by Joseph Almog, John Perry, and Howard Wettstein. Rather charmingly, the published version retains many of the idiosyncracies of the still slightly rough circulated version, including progress notes in square brackets, such as '[This section is not yet written. What follows is a rough outline of what is to come]' and '[My current inclination is to drop this whole section from the final draft.]' It also contains (on page 489) the classic line 'I believe my theory of demonstratives to be uncontrovertable and largely uncontroversial,' followed, in a footnote, by the wise qualification 'Not everything I assert is part of my theory.' Despite these touches of whimsical humour, the manuscript as a whole is quite technical and would be hard going for a beginner.

My rather informal explanation of the semantics of bound variable pronouns is very distantly descended from the treatment of bound variables in Alfred Tarski's classic paper 'The concept of truth in formalized languages', pages 152–278 of his book *Logic, Semantics, and Metamathematics* (Oxford University Press, 1983, 2nd edition), translated by J.H. Woodger. The paper first appeared in Polish in 1933. It is rather technical.

The problem of donkey anaphora was apparently first discussed by the medieval logicians. Walter Burleigh, for example, writing in the early fourteenth century, considered the example *Omnis homo habens asinum videt illum* ('Every man who has a donkey sees it', *De puritate artis logicae tractatus longior*, paragraphs 128–32). The beating was introduced when the English philosopher Peter Geach turned the example into *Any man who owns a donkey beats it* on page 117 of his book *Reference and Generality* (Cornell University Press, 1962). This is still fairly old, though not nearly as old as the example itself. Geach was responsible for introducing these examples to modern philosophers and linguists. I owe most of this mini-history of donkey anaphora to Pieter Seuren's book *The Logic of Language* (Oxford University Press, 2010), page 300.

Descriptive indexicals were discovered by the American linguist Geoff Nunberg. See his article 'Indexicality and deixis', *Linguistics and Philosophy* 16: 1–43, 1993. The example about the Pope being an Italian, credited to Nunberg, actually comes from François Recanati's paper 'Deixis and anaphora', pages 286–316 of *Semantics versus Pragmatics* (Oxford University Press, 2005), edited by Zoltan Szabó. These technical works are aimed at professional linguists and philosophers.

The quotation from J.K Rowling is from page 279 of *Harry Potter and the Deathly Hallows* (Bloomsbury, 2007). The observation that pronouns can take on quantifier phrase meanings in this way has not been published before as far as I know.

The example about the Saturday before classes start is from page 29 of the article of Nunberg's just referred to.

Reams have been written about *It's raining*. As far as I know, the example originates in John Perry's article 'Thought without representation', *Supplementary Proceedings of the Aristotelian Society* 60 (1986): 263–283. The example *Everyone was sick* comes from Stephen Neale's book *Descriptions*, cited above in connection with Chapter 5, pages 94–5. And *I haven't eaten* is discussed on pages 135–6 of Kent Bach's article 'Conversational implicature', *Mind & Language* 9 (1994): 124–162. The theory about topic situations comes from Barwise and Perry's *Situations and Attitudes*, cited above in connection with Chapter 4, page 161. Influential objections to this theory along the lines given in the main text were put forward by Dag Westerståhl and Scott Soames: in Westerståhl's article 'Determiners and context sets', pages 45–71 of *Generalized Quantifiers in Natural Language* (Foris, 1985), edited by Johan van Benthem and Alice ter Meulen; and in Soames's article 'Incomplete definite descriptions', *Notre Dame Journal of Formal Logic* 27 (1986): 349–375. The example about the sleepers and the research assistant is from Soames. Covert indexicals in the syntax of the kind described here go back at least to Kai von Fintel's PhD dissertation *Restrictions on Quantifier Domains* (University of Massachusetts at Amherst, 1994). With the possible exception of

Neale's book, as noted above, none of this material is particularly accessible to beginners.

Jason Stanley's position can be appreciated by reading some or all of the essays in his book *Language in Context* (Oxford University Press, 2007). Sperber and Wilson's classic work is *Relevance: Communication and Cognition* (Blackwell, 1986). These two volumes would be fairly accessible to the reader of the current book, although the going would be rough in places.

Smith v. United States (91-8674), 508 U.S. 223 (1993). The case is briefly discussed on pages 23-4 of Antonin Scalia's book *A Matter of Interpretation: Federal Courts and the Law* (Princeton University Press, 1998). This is a fascinating and highly accessible guide to one justice's philosophy of legal interpretation. When I say that philosophers are starting to work on the issue of implicit content and legal interpretation, I am thinking chiefly of Stephen Neale, most of whose work on this subject is unfortunately unpublished. But there is a brief discussion of this case at the start of Neale's essay 'On location', pages 251-393 of *Situating Semantics: Essays on the Philosophy of John Perry* (MIT Press, 2007), edited by Michael O'Rourke and Corey Washington. This essay, which is mostly about *It's raining*, would be partly accessible to someone who has read the present book, but it would be rough going at times.

H.P. Grice's classic account of implicature is 'Logic and conversation', pages 41-58 of *Syntax and Semantics, 3: Speech Acts* (Academic Press, 1975), edited by P. Cole and J. Morgan. Some of this paper, as the title indicates, deals with the meanings of logical operators; but most of it would be quite accessible to the reader of the current book who has no more logical knowledge.

The full transcript of the speech of Hillary Clinton's quoted in this chapter can be found at http://transcripts.cnn.com/TRANSCRIPTS/0801/06/cnr.01.html.

Chapter 8

The Wittgenstein quotation is proposition 5.6 of the *Tractatus Logico-Philosophicus* in the translation of C.K. Ogden (Routledge & Kegan Paul, 1922).

The quotation from Whorf can be found on page 213 of *Language, Thought and Reality: Selected Writings of Benjamin Lee Whorf* (MIT Press, 1956), edited by John B. Carroll. Interestingly enough, Sapir used exactly the same adverb in one of his hedges on the subject: 'We see and hear and otherwise experience *very largely* as we do because the language habits of our community predispose certain choices of interpretation' (my emphasis; page 210 of Sapir's article 'The status of linguistics as a science', *Language* 5(4), 1929, pages 207–14). Sapir and Whorf's writings on this subject are highly accessible.

Greg Murphy writes about dust bunnies on pages 389–90 of his book *The Big Book of Concepts*, cited above in connection with Chapter 1.

Susan Schaller's account of giving language to Ildefonso can be found in her lucid and accessible book *A Man Without Words* (Summit Books, 1991). Karen Wynn's experiment was published in her paper 'Addition and subtraction in human infants', *Nature* 358, 1992, pages 749–50. This paper is slightly technical, but should be mostly accessible to readers of the current book. I was alerted to the publications by Schaller and Wynn by reading the discussion of the Sapir-Whorf hypothesis in Chapter 3 of Steven Pinker's *The Language Instinct* (William Morrow, 1994), where I was also reminded of the relevance of Newspeak; in the unlikely event that you have not read this magnificently entertaining and persuasive book, I recommend that you do so soon.

The literature on Pirahã is already quite large and involves topics other than the number system. Amongst other highlights, Daniel Everett has alleged that Pirahã does not have recursion, the syntactic device that enables users of every other known human language to embed sentences inside other sentences (as subordinate clauses). But the literature is in general fascinating and more accessible than many technical publications. I estimate that the following works would be mostly accessible to the reader of the present book, although the going would be rough occasionally. Peter Gordon's article is 'Numerical cognition without words: evidence from Amazonia', *Science* 306, 2004, pages 496–99. The study by Michael Frank, Daniel Everett, Evelina Fedorenko, and Edward Gibson is 'Number as a cognitive technology: evidence from Pirahã language and cognition', *Cognition* 108, 2008, pages 819–24. Doubts about the direction of causation were first expressed in print by Daniel Casasanto in a letter to *Science*: 'Crying Whorf', *Science* 307, 2005, pages 1721–2 (followed by a reply by Gordon). Daniel Everett's book *Don't sleep, there are snakes* (Profile Books, 2008) is particularly engaging and accessible. (I disagree with some of what he has to say, though, as I mention in the main text.) Everett's main scholarly publication on Pirahã language and culture, including the immediacy of experience principle, is 'Cultural constraints on grammar and cognition in Pirahã: another look at the design features of human language', *Current Anthropology* 46(4), 2005, pages 621–34; it is followed by commentary by several other scholars and a reply by Everett. The work cited by Nevins, Pesetsky, and Rodrigues, in spite of its relevance for Gordon's claims, is mainly devoted to criticizing Everett's work: 'Pirahã exceptionality: a reassessment', *Language* 85(2), 2009, pages 355–404. Everett replied in 'Pirahã culture and grammar: a response to some criticisms', *Language* 85(2), 2009, pages 405–42; the formulation of the immediacy of experience principle given in the text is taken from this article. Nevins, Pesetsky, and Rodrigues responded in turn with 'Evidence and argumentation: a reply to Everett (2009)', *Language* 85(3), 2009, pages 671–81.

I owe the quotation from Andrei Makine to a lecture by Lera Boroditsky before the Long Now Foundation given on 26 October 2010. It is available online at http://fora.tv/2010/10/26/Lera_Boroditsky_How_Language_Shapes_Thought. The paper by Boroditsky, Schmidt, and Phillips is 'Sex, syntax, and semantics', pages 61–79 of *Language in mind: advances in the study of language and thought* (MIT Press, 2003), edited by Dedre Gentner and Susan Goldin-Meadow. Boroditsky's article on Mandarin and English is 'Does language shape thought? Mandarin and English speakers' conceptions of time' in *Cognitive Psychology* 43: 1–22, 2001. The first of these publications is quite accessible; the second is rather more technical. The quotation from Steven Pinker is from a Boston Globe article from 18 November 2003, 'She explores the world of language and thought', available online at http://www-psych.stanford.edu/~lera/press/globe2003.html.

Index